FROM ME TO YOU

SONGS THE BEATLES COVERED
AND SONGS THEY GAVE AWAY

BY BRIAN SOUTHALL

The publishers make no representation, express or implied,
with regard to the accuracy of the information contained in
this publication and cannot accept any responsibility in law
for any errors or omissions. Whilst we have attempted to
check the accuracy at the time of going to press, the access
to locations, opening hours of events and premises, and
any other details, may change beyond our control. Where
locations are private residences, we particularly ask all readers
to respect absolutely the privacy of those who live there.

The publishers have made every reasonable effort to trace
the copyright owners of any and all of the material in this
book. In the event of an omission, the publishers will be
pleased to hear from anyone who has not been appropriately
acknowledged, and to make a correction in any future reprints
and editions.

The right of Brian Southall to be identified as author of this
Work has been asserted by him in accordance with sections 77
and 78 of the Copyright, Designs and Patents Act 1988.

This edition © Red Planet Publishing Ltd 2014
Text © Brian Southall 2014

ISBN: 978 1 9059 5923 5

Printed in the UK by CPI

The paper used in this book is FSC certified and totally
chlorine-free. FSC (the Forest Stewardship Council) is an
international network to promote responsible management
of the world's forests.

www.redplanetzone.com

Contents 3

INTRODUCTION   PAGE 5

COVERED AND CAPTURED ON VINYL   PAGE 15
Carl Perkins, Larry Williams, Chuck Berry, Little Richard, The Shirelles,
Arthur Alexander, The Cookies, Dr Feelgood, The Donays, Buddy Holly,
The Isley Brothers, Peggy Lee, The Marvelettes, Buck Owens, Smokey
Robinson, Barrett Strong, Gene Vincent, Lenny Welch

COVERS FROM THE LIVE SET LIST   PAGE 63
Carol, Johnny B Goode, Little Queenie, Sweet Little Sixteen, Too Much
Monkey Business, Glad All Over, Lend Me Your Comb, Sure To Fall, Your
True Love , I Got A Woman, I Forgot To Remember To Forget, I'm Going
To Sit Right Down And Cry Over You, That's All Right (Mama), Searchin',
Three Cool Cats, Young Blood, C'mon Everybody, Hallelujah, Twenty,
Flight Rock, Lucille, Ooh My Soul, Be-Bop-A-Lula, Dance In The Street,
Down Town Strutters' Ball, Nothin' Shakin' (But The Leaves On The
Trees), (I Do The) Shimmy Shimmy, Crying Waiting Hoping, Clarabella,
Well Baby Please Don't Go, Hippy Hippy Shake, Red Sails In The Sunset

SONGS THE BEATLES GAVE AWAY   PAGE 93
Billy J Kramer & The Dakotas: I'll Be On My Way, Bad To Me, I'll Keep
You Satisfied, From A Window. **Peter & Gordon:** A World Without Love,
Nobody I Know, I Don't Want To See You, Woman. **Cilla Black:** Love Of
The Loved , It's For You, Step Inside Love. **The Fourmost:** Hello Little
Girl, I'm In Love. **The Applejacks:** Like Dreamers Do. **Badfinger:** Come
And Get It. **Chris Barber & his Jazz Band:** Catcall. **The Black Dyke
Mills Band:** Thingumybob. **Mary Hopkin:** Goodbye. **Jackie Lomax:**
Sour Milk Sea. **George Martin Orchestra:** Love In The Open Air. **Jotta
Herre/Carlos Mende:** Penina. **PJ Proby:** That Means A Lot. **Tommy
Quickly:** Tip Of My Tongue. **The Strangers with Mike Shannon:** One
And One Is Two. **Doris Troy:** Ain't She Cute

BEATLES COVERS UNCOVERED   PAGE 117
Across The Universe, And I Love Her, Can't Buy Me Love, Come
Together, Day Tripper, From Me To You, Eleanor Rigby, Get Back, Got To
Get You Into My Life, A Hard Day's Night, Help! Here Comes The Sun,
Hey Jude, I Am The Walrus, I Saw Her Standing There, In My Life, Let It
Be, Lucy In The Sky With Diamonds, Michelle, Ob-La-Di-Ob-La-Da,
She's Leaving Home, Something, We Can Work It Out, With A Little
Help From My Friends, Yesterday

From Me To You

This book takes a detailed look at the songs covered – both on record and on stage – by The Beatles after they officially came into being in 1960. And what they all have in common is a special place among the list of favourites songs spanning the most demanding, most creative and most successful period in the group's time together.

Placed alongside these 'non-Beatle' songs – most of which are American in origin – is a varied and fascinating selection of the group's own compositions which, over the years, have been recorded by other artists.

The title – in the context of this collection of songs The Beatles covered both on record and on stage plus a selection of cover version of Beatles' songs

6 From Me To You

– says it all. In fact the title 'From Me To You' was taken from the name of the reader's letters column in the music paper New Musical Express. Yet it somehow sums up the idea of The Beatles delivering their music for the rest of us to enjoy.

But it also encompasses the music four aspiring young musicians, living in the North of England in the somewhat grimy and underprivileged Britain of the 1950s, took into their hearts and heads in their search for both songs and inspiration.

Rock 'n' roll, rhythm and blues, soul, stage shows, film soundtracks and even country music were all delivered to John Paul George and Ringo from a host of mainly American performers whose records played a major part in the musical education of arguably the greatest group of musicians the world has ever seen and heard.

And, similarly, a bewildering assortment of artists have enthusiastically collected up the songs The Beatles wrote (and released) and put their own individual stamp on them before once again sending them out into the world.

Perhaps surprisingly the song 'From Me To You' was not credited, as most of their Beatle songs were, to Lennon and McCartney. On its release in 1963, it became the last Beatles' single to be issued with the credit McCartney-Lennon … and it was one of the few compositions to be genuinely co-written by Paul and John.

'From Me To You' was The Beatles' third single and is acknowledged as their first 'official' number one hit – despite suggestions that 'Please Please Me' topped at least one of charts of the day. And according to George Harrison it was a crucial release. "'From Me To You' was really important because that put the stamp on it."

Written on a tour bus taking The Beatles and top of the bill star Helen Shapiro from York to Shrewsbury at the end of February 1963, Lennon recalled that writing 'From Me To You' began as a half-hearted affair. "We weren't taking ourselves seriously – just fooling around on the guitar – when we began to get a good melody line and we really started to work on it."

According to McCartney the song was a genuine joint effort. "'From Me To You' was both of us, very much together", he says but it also signalled the last time any of the joint compositions released as Beatles' singles would be credited as McCartney/Lennon songs. The group's first single 'Love Me Do' and 'P.S. I Love You' (both Paul songs) were credited as Lennon-McCartney while the follow up 'Please Please Me' and 'Ask Me Why' appeared on the label as McCartney-Lennon songs.

When it came to 'From Me To You' – and the B-side 'Thank You Girl '– Paul won a battle but lost the war to John and manager Brian Epstein. "John had the stronger personality and I think he fixed things with Brian before I got there. They all said Lennon/McCartney sounds better, it has a better ring. I had to say 'Oh all right, sod it!'" However, Paul won a further battle when all eight of their joint compositions on the *Please Please Me* album were credited as McCartney-Lennon.

Nowadays it goes without question that John Lennon and Paul McCartney are the most famous, the most successful and among the most talented songwriters to emerge during the 20th century. They not only took the craft of writing popular music to new heights but also changed the outlook for a host of ambitious, emerging new artists in the frenzy that was the swingin' sixties.

However, there were established rock and pop writers before the two most creative members of The Beatles took over at the controls, and artists such as **Chuck Berry**,

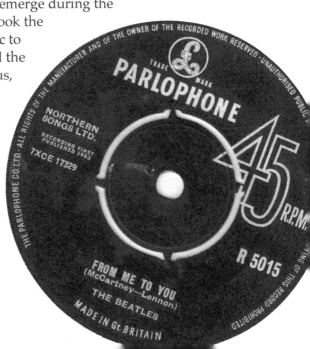

Little Richard, Buddy Holly, Carl Perkins, Larry Williams, Arthur Alexander and **Smokey Robinson** stood shoulder to shoulder with talented composing teams such as **Jerry Leiber & Mike Stoller** and **Gerry Goffin & Carole King** as the people The Beatles admired and whose songs they chose to record.

Between them, these talents – along with a host of other professional songwriters including Neil Sedaka & Howard Greenfield, Otis Blackwell, Doc Pumas & Mort Shulman, Burt Bacharach & Hal David, Barry Mann & Cynthia Weil and Jeff Barry & Ellie Greenwich – supplied the material which a multitude of artists, white and black, male and female, American and British, turned into the golden soundtrack of a generation.

Before The Beatles truly arrived in early 1963, with their own collection of clever new pop songs alongside classic American rock 'n' pop creations that influenced their very being let alone their musical taste buds, it had been the task of the 'songwriter' to provide the 'artist' with the hits.

And working in New York's Brill Building and London's Denmark Street – both areas ultimately nicknamed Tin Pan Alley – there were enough writers and songs to meet the demands of major non-composing stars such as Elvis Presley, Cliff Richard, Helen Shapiro, Adam Faith, Billy Fury, Bobby Darin, Pat Boone, Connie Francis, Brenda Lee and groups like The Drifters, The Coasters, The Crystals and The Shirelles.

Of course there were acts 'across the water' such as Ray Charles, The Everly

Brothers, Roy Orbison, Johnny Cash, Jerry Lee Lewis and Eddie Cochran who both performed and composed but, in Britain in the early 1960s, songwriters gathered in cafes and pubs in London's Soho district to offer their latest wares to music publishers hungry to find the next big hit.

The arrival of The Beatles – John and Paul together with George Harrison and ultimately Ringo Starr – with their ability to both play and write proved an inspiration to every new group and prompted the likes of Mick Jagger & Keith Richard, Pete Townshend, Ray Davies and Eric Clapton amongst others to try their hand at song writing.

But still John and Paul, with George hanging doggedly on to their coat tails, had to be moved and motivated in order to experiment and test their skills as lyricists and tunesmiths until they eventually emerged as composers of the highest calibre.

It is for that reason that the artists and song writers highlighted earlier in **bold** find themselves lumped together. They were among the earliest and greatest influences on The Beatles in their formative years in Liverpool.

Their music and songs arrived in Britain's most important northern port courtesy of the sailors who returned with records collected in the States and tunes heard on US radio stations where pop music was a well established ingredient in the fight for listeners.

As The Beatles grew out of The Quarrymen, Johnny & the Moondogs, The Beatals and The Silver Beetles to finally take a name that was adopted in honour of the group which featured their ultimate hero – Buddy Holly and his Crickets – so they worked these 'new' American songs into their live act.

And they weren't the only ones who picked up on the new music of America and quickly made it part of their stage show. The Rolling Stones, The Kinks, The Animals, The Searchers, The Hollies and Cliff Richard and The Shadows were all at it as Shadows' guitarist Bruce Welch recalls, "What we all did was play the rock 'n' roll that came from America. In fact we and other acts were doing it

12 From Me To You

before The Beatles broke. We all had the same heroes – Elvis, Chuck Berry, Little Richard, Buddy Holly and The Everlys – so we would cover all their songs and do them on stage."

10CC member Graham Gouldman played with local Manchester bands The Whirlwinds and The Mockingbirds in the early 1960s before writing hits for The Yardbirds, The Hollies and Herman's Hermits and he has a similar recollection of the live circuit.

"There was almost like one repertoire that all the bands did. You could hear different versions of the same songs from different bands – all the R&B classics mainly – and it didn't seem to make any difference."

Finally, when the long-awaited and much coveted recording contract finally arrived in 1962, The Beatles saw their opportunity to include many of the same songs on their albums. But, if they had assembled a larger catalogue of Lennon/McCartney compositions – or even a few more Harrison songs – in those early days, it's debatable whether they would still have recorded and issued the bulk of those 'covers' between 1963 and 1965.

But the importance of The Beatles pricking up their ears to the music of America and learning from it was confirmed by George Martin in his autobiography *All You Need Is Ears* when he said, "We re-exported American music back to America. They would listen to American records, lift phrases and work out how they'd want to do it."

American rock singer Alice Cooper remains a huge Beatles fan and recalls one of the reasons why they got to him. "One of the things I was really attracted to by The Beatles was when they did rock 'n' roll. Chuck Berry, Little Richard – stuff like that was what Paul and John could both really do and you could see they both had 50s influences. They really do show their early rock influences in those songs they covered."

And even former Sex Pistol Glen Matlock, who wasn't even a teenager when the first Beatles' records came out, acknowledges the influence they had on his listening pleasure in later life. "I do like their cover versions and through listening to The Beatles I got turned on to people like Arthur Alexander and The Isley Brothers which isn't such a bad thing."

But one American singer and songwriter was seemingly not so impressed with what he heard from The Beatles in those early days. Gene Pitney was in the recording studio in America when he first heard an acetate of the *Please Please Me* album and his first reaction was extreme to say the least. "I have to say I hated it", said the man who played piano on the Rolling Stones' first album and tragically died during his 2006 UK tour.

"It was a lot of covers of things I thought were sacred and I didn't like the way they were done. To me they were like the white man's version of some great blues songs", was his view at the time although he later added, "But of course I was proved totally wrong."

Most of the songs which ended up on record were numbers they played on stage in youth centres, town halls, clubs and theatres around the UK – not forgetting Germany's collection of seedy venues – but they did leave some classic songs on the ballroom floor including one Chuck Berry composition which survived in their live set for four years but never made it onto any official Beatles release.

Similarly, they only ever officially recorded one song by their ultimate hero Buddy Holly despite covering his songs regularly from the late 50s until the early 60s, while music from the likes of Eddie Cochran, Gene Vincent, Elvis Presley, Jerry Lee Lewis, Ray Charles, The Coasters and

14 From Me To You

The Drifters never ever made it into the studio although some songs did appear on various live and early pre-Beatles releases.

So where do we start with the list of songs which John, Paul, George and Ringo put down on vinyl? It was a question which required some thought in order to reflect the part the songs, the performers and the writers played in the working life of The Beatles from 1960 onwards and were so important to them that they included them in their enduring and all conquering catalogue of recordings.

Which means that we start – in alphabetical order – with four men who over the years contributed most songs to The Beatles' in-studio repertoire (plus a host of numbers that featured in their live shows over the years) and, as a result, have a place in rock history as the writers whose compositions perhaps most impressed the world's most successful and famous group.

Covered and captured on vinyl

Reflecting on the music which The Beatles listened to and loved the most, John Lennon once observed that rock 'n' roll was "the music that brought me from the provinces to the world." While the 25 songs they didn't write but chose to record, span almost every genre of music, there was, again according to John, just one style that was at the very heart and soul of the group's influences. "I don't know where we'd have been without rock 'n' roll."

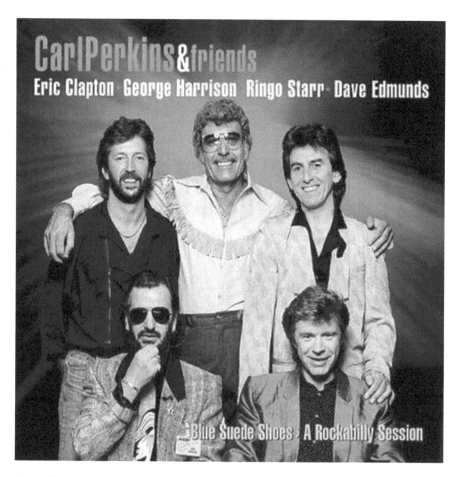

Carl Perkins

CARL PERKINS was born in Tennessee in 1932 and initially formed a band with his two brothers before signing to the legendary Memphis-based Sun Records, owned by Sam Phillips, where he joined Elvis Presley both on the label and on tour.

He is best remembered for writing and recording the rock classic

'Blue Suede Shoes' in 1955, which reached number 2 in the US chart and was a top ten hit in the UK – his only British chart entry. He moved on from Sun, toured the UK and recorded a host of country-influenced songs which brought him only modest commercial success.

Nevertheless his country/blues/rockabilly guitar playing and song writing skills established him as a major influence on a whole string of new acts including The Beatles, who included many of Perkins' songs in their live shows including the iconic 'Blue Suede Shoes', 'Sure To Fall', 'Glad All Over' and 'Gone Gone Gone'.

For John, Perkins held a special place in his musical apprenticeship. "There have only been two great albums that I listened to all the way through when I was sixteen. One was Carl Perkins' first or second, I can't remember which, and one was Elvis' first. Those are the only ones on which I really enjoyed every track."

While John was a long-time fan, Perkins ended up recording the duet 'Get It' with Paul in 1981 for the *Tug Of War* album and also performed live with both George and Ringo during his lengthy career.

Perkins died in 1998 and on his last album *Go Cat Go* he featured each of The Beatles – John's live version of 'Blue Suede Shoes'; Paul singing 'My Old Friend', which Perkins had written as a tribute to The Beatles bass player; Ringo's offering of 'Matchbox' and George's home studio version of 'Distance Makes No Difference'.

George's special fondness for Perkins and his music led to the former Beatle performing at the American singer's funeral in Tennessee, which perhaps served as some sort

18 From Me To You

of thank you for the songs The Beatles covered both on stage and on record.

'Everybody's Trying To Be My Baby' came from Perkins's 1958 *Teen Beat* album and was featured in The Beatles' live sets for four years between 1961 and 1965 – it oddly disappeared from the 1963 shows – and eventually found its way onto the *Beatles For Sale* album.

With George taking a heavily echo-laden lead vocal, the track was recorded in Abbey Road late in the day on October 18 1964. It was done in one take as the band wound up a day off from their UK tour by recording seven new tracks.

* In his original Perkins produces an Elvis-style vocal with loads of echo over a simple rocking beat and multiple guitar breaks and the whole thing runs out at a very short 1.53 seconds.

* Adding a full 30 seconds to the original, The Beatles offer their own intro featuring guitar and vocal interchanges with George offering one of his best vocal performances despite the echo. He also adds in some effective guitar breaks in a much faster and livelier cover version.

NME writer Derek Johnson pointed out in his November 13 1964 review of the album that, "'Everybody's Trying To Be My Baby' is the Carl Perkins number you may have heard the boys work on stage. A medium fast shaker spotlighting George as vocalist, it has an insistent rhythm."

'Honey Don't' was originally the flip-side to the massive million-selling hit 'Blue Suede Shoes' and became a regular in Beatles' shows between 1962 and 1965. While John took the lead vocal at the outset, the spotlight switched to Ringo in 1963 and it became one of the drummer's featured moments on tour.

Speaking years later Ringo explained that the song went back to his pre-Beatles days. "We all knew 'Honey Don't', it was one of those songs that every band in Liverpool played. I used to love country music and country rock. I'd had my own show with Rory Storm when I would do five or six minutes. So singing and performing wasn't new to me, it was a case of finding a vehicle for me with The Beatles. That's why we did it on *Beatles For Sale*. It was comfortable. And I was finally getting one track on a record, my little featured spot."

As George once pointed out, including the two Carl Perkins songs on *Beatles For Sale* made life that bit easier for The Beatles in the midst of touring, recording and writing. "For this album we rehearsed only the new ones. Songs like 'Honey Don't' and 'Everybody's Trying To Be My Baby' we'd played live so often that we only had to get a sound on them and do them."

In fact the track was recorded on October 26 1964 as the band was getting to the end of the 27 date twice-nightly UK tour with Mary Wells and Sounds Incorporated. Recording began at 4.30 in the afternoon and Ringo completed his role as lead vocalist in five takes.

* Perkins begins his version with guitar leading into a simple bass/drum combination to create a pacy feel as the main man throws in some fine guitar slapping and an effective solo alongside his trademark rock vocal.

* The Beatles repeat the same guitar intro before Ringo's vocal takes over. He sounds unconvincing at first but gradually warms to his task and brings George into the song with a shout of "rock on George – one time for me" and the guitarist obliges with two fine guitar breaks.

In his book *The Beatles Album File and Complete Discography*, Jeff Russell's assessment is that "Ringo eases his way through with his own singalong style" while *Melody Maker's* October 1964 review of the album says simply, "Ringo singing … and there is great guitar boogie going on."

NME had a bit more to say with Johnson writing, "'Honey Don't' was written by Carl Perkins, with Ringo

handling the repetitive and compulsive lyric, set to a walking pace rhythm with electronic plucking."

The song – covered by a host of rock and country artists including Ronnie Hawkins and Johnny Rivers – was also eventually re-recorded by Ringo Starr & His All Starr Band, featuring Dr John, Billy Preston, Nils Lofgren, Joe Walsh, Jim Keltner, Rick Danko and Levon Helm, for their 1990 live album.

'Matchbox' was originally thought by some to be a re-working of a traditional blues number recorded by Lead Belly and Blind Lemon Jefferson. Perkins' up-dated version was recorded in the Sun Studios with Jerry Lee Lewis on piano on December 4 1956, just ahead of Elvis Presley and Johnny Cash visiting. The subsequent impromptu jam session led to the famed *Million Dollar Quartet* tapes which were finally released after Presley's death in 1977.

The Beatles featured the song in their live show between 1961 and 1962 and original drummer Pete Best was the chosen lead vocalist until John took over. Finally Ringo made the song his own and it was featured on the best-selling 1964 EP *Long Tall Sally* and as a B-side to the US single 'Slow Down'.

The Beatles went to Abbey Road Studios on June 1 1964 soon after returning from holiday following the filming of *A Hard Day's Night*. Intending to record the non-soundtrack side of the new album, The Beatles decided to set aside any spare tracks for the planned EP and Perkins' song was first up.

With Ringo on vocals, the afternoon session took on a special feel as Perkins arrived to witness The Beatles record the first of their three cover versions of his songs which would keep him in royalties for the rest of his life.

With Ringo opting to sing and drum at the same time, the song was done in five takes and Perkins recalled it as "a magic time", and even claimed that the group also recorded a version of 'Blue Suede Shoes' on the same day although nothing has ever been heard or was ever logged in the studio session sheets.

* Perkins brings in an early rocking piano behind a vocal that again sounds remarkably like an Elvis impersonation. He adds a couple of well picked guitar solos and the whole thing bounces along to finish in 2.06 seconds.

* The Beatles choose to put Ringo's rougher and louder vocal, with just a touch of echo, over an insistent guitar and pounding drum beat. George's guitar breaks follow the lines of Perkins' original but the band opt to end the whole thing a little earlier at 1.56 seconds on a resounding guitar note.

In his original sleeve notes for the EP, The Beatles' press officer Derek Taylor concludes that Ringo makes the song "his very own" before adding, "He sings little but well, which is better than rotten and often."

Larry Williams

LARRY WILLIAMS is the least famous and arguably the least successful of the great influences on The Beatles. Born in New Orleans, Williams started out as a chauffeur to musician Lloyd Price before turning his hand to song writing and recording and, between 1957 and 1958, he penned the classic rock 'n' roll tracks 'Short Fat Fanny', 'High School Dance' and 'Bony Moronie'.

All three were US hits and the million-selling 'Short Fat Fanny' and 'Bony Moronie' both hit the UK charts during the same period and

also became regulars in The Beatles' shows between1960 and 1962 when they gave way to the band's growing collection of original compositions.

Groomed by the Speciality label as a successor to Little Richard, piano-playing Williams' career never took off again after his late 1950s successes although he continued to tour despite being jailed for drug offences in 1960. In 1980 he was found dead in his Los Angeles home with a gunshot wound to the head, but three of his songs had by then been selected and recorded by The Beatles.

'Dizzy Miss Lizzy' was not one of Williams' major chart hits but it still established itself as a rock 'n' roll favourite in the late 1950s and early 1960s as the third of his trio of songs about girlfriends – following on from the unflattering 'Short Fat Fanny' and 'Bony Moronie'.

All three songs were part of Beatles live shows but 'Dizzy Miss Lizzy' was the most popular, being featured for over four years, from 1960 to 1962, and then reappearing in 1965 when it was also included on the group's *Help* album.

When The Beatles did the last of their live BBC radio shows in June 1965 it was again on the song list, and the recording from their August 30 1965 concert also made it onto the *Live At Hollywood Bowl* album.

It was recorded in Abbey Road during the evening of May 10 1965 when two tracks specially made for the US market were laid down. John took the lead as he did on stage and the song was completed in a total of seven takes.

* Williams offers up a strained slightly forced vocal with a brass section pumping out the intro behind his guitar. After a brief guitar break, Williams' pounding piano backs his singing through to a big note ending at 2.10 sec.

* The Beatles simplified the intro to feature just a guitar and John's vocal is more powerful and a touch frenetic compared to the original. George offers up some simple yet effective guitar as the song moves along at a faster pace but ends up 40 seconds longer than Williams' effort.

In his *Complete Guide To The Music Of The Beatles* John Robertson wrote that "Lennon cruised through the vocal like the natural rock 'n' roller he was" on the last full cover version of a song (ever) to be included on an official Beatles album, while Russell concluded that the song was close to the original arrangement with "some oohs and aahs to give a live sound."

The two leading music papers of the day were divided in their opinion of the Beatles version of Williams' rock classic. *NME*'s Derek Johnson wrote in the July 23 1965 issue, "John semi-shouts this raving rocker, aided by strident, raucous twangs from George and Ringo almost going berserk", while Melody Maker concluded, "Strangely 'Dizzy Miss Lizzy' sounds a bit of a let-down after 'Yesterday' (the song which preceded it on the album). It's straight rock 'n' roll and sounds a bit meandering."

In addition to appearing on *Help*, the track recorded specially for America also made it onto Capitol's *Beatles VI* compilation which became the band's fifth US number one album.

'Bad Boy' was released by Williams in 1959 and, while it failed to chart, it did register with The Beatles who featured the song in the live shows between 1960 and 1962 with John again taking the lead.

At one point George explained that the decision as to who would sing the lead vocal when it came to cover versions was down to "who had the biggest ego and who shouted the loudest." He also added, "John was the main man really. He was the oldest and probably the best

vocalist as well. There weren't any rules. It was just the way things evolved naturally."

The song was the other track recorded for the US market together with 'Dizzy Miss Lizzy' and featured John's vocal alongside Paul on electric piano, John on organ and Ringo on tambourine on the four takes completed on May 10 1965.

* Williams starts out with a big brass intro before moving into a slight novelty theme by throwing in deep bass lines asking "Who's a bad boy" every now and then. The twanging guitar break runs over some screams but the song never really gets going.

* The four Beatles go straight into the intro before John comes in with a much more straightforward and effective rocking vocal with no novelty lines and some nifty guitar licks.

The song made it on to the same *Beatles VI* album for America but was never included on any official UK studio album or EP and only finally saw the light of day on the 1966 release *A Collection of Beatles Oldies*. Covered by Rush, it was also included as the title track on Ringo Starr's 1978 solo album which was made up of cover versions.

'Slow Down' was the song Williams put on the B-side of his 1958 single release of 'Dizzy Miss Lizzy' and soon after it found its way onto The Beatles' set list for live dates between 1960 and 1962.

Recorded in six takes in Abbey Road on June 1 1964, the song features John on lead vocal alongside producer Martin's piano which was added to the track three days later.

* Williams sets things off with a crashing 30 second piano intro before his rough rock 'n' roll vocal comes in to take things along at a smart pace. A long raucous piano and sax break comes in before it all runs to an end at 2.43 seconds.

* Martin's effective piano kicks things off for The Beatles before John's harsher and more urgent vocal comes in. A pounding beat and single scream lead into a 25 second guitar and piano break and the tracks ends at a slightly longer 2.53 seconds on a single guitar note and a final "whooaah'.

It was issued in the US as the B-side of 'Matchbox', another track from the same UK EP *Long Tall Sally* where, in his original sleeve notes, PR man Taylor describes the track as "a moody rocker, note-perfect product of the Beatles early performances in Liverpool's Cavern."

Chuck Berry

CHUCK BERRY, who was born in either San Jose, California or St Louis, Missouri in 1926 (most records suggest California although Berry says that Missouri was where he was raised), began his musical career leading a blues trio before joining up with the hugely influential Chess Records in Chicago in 1955 and recording his debut disc 'Maybellene'.

While his records did bring him significant chart success, his enormous influence on a whole generation of emerging young musicians came from his songwriting and live performances. Even though his career was interrupted in 1962 by a two year jail sentence for crossing a US state line with an under age girl, Berry emerged to find that a host of new British bands were regularly performing his songs, both on stage and on record.

In *The Beatles Anthology*, John spoke about the influence Berry had on his music and his life.

26 From Me To You

Describing him as "one of the all-time great poets; a rock poet", he went on to explain the impact made by Berry's songs. "In the fifties when people were virtually singing about nothing Chuck Berry was writing social-comment songs with incredible metre to the lyrics. When I hear good rock 'n' roll, good rock of the calibre of Chuck Berry, I just fall apart and I have no other interest in life."

He went further and even suggested, "If you tried to give rock 'n' roll another name you might call it Chuck Berry", while his song writing partner Paul gave a little insight into how the early Beatles were influenced by the man born Charles Berry. "We'd go up to John's bedroom with his little record player and listen to Chuck Berry records, trying to learn them."

In fact they learnt them so well that between 1960 and 1966 The Beatles included more songs in their live shows by Berry than by any other composer. Tracks such as 'Johnny B. Goode', 'Maybellene', 'Sweet Little Sixteen', 'Carol', 'Memphis Tennessee', 'Reelin' And Rockin'' and 'Too Much Monkey Business' were all regulars and played a major part in Berry's rehabilitation into the international music business after his jail term, as he later acknowledged – albeit a little begrudgingly – in his autobiography *Chuck Berry*.

"The media quoted their (The Beatles) mentions of some of my songs that they had recorded, which naturally was a great help to my then 'sleeping' repertoire," he said although he was more forthcoming after John apparently named him as one of his heroes. "This was one of the most stimulating statements that had ever been bestowed upon me," he wrote.

While it is freely acknowledged that The Beatles' 'Back In The USSR' was hugely influenced by Berry's 1959 top 40 hit 'Back In The USA', it is a number from two years earlier which heads up the list of his songs which The Beatles covered on record.

'Rock And Roll Music' was a US top ten hit for Berry in 1957 and was virtually an ever-present on The Beatles' set list every year from 1960 until their final tour, which ended in San Francisco's Candlestick

Park in August 1966. By that time The Beatles were featuring more of their own material and 'Rock And Roll Music' was one of only two songs by other writers that they performed in that last year when they toured West Germany, Japan, the Philippines and North America.

While the likes of The Beach Boys, Humble Pie and REO Speedwagon recorded versions of the song in the 1970s, with Manic Street Preachers adding a 2003 cover, it was The Beatles who put one of the earliest versions down on vinyl in 1964 on their fourth album *Beatles For Sale*.

It was recorded in just one take in Abbey Road Studios on the evening of October 18 1964 with Lennon taking lead vocals and producer George Martin joining John and Paul at the piano to add some serious rock 'n' roll keyboard to the mix.

* *On his original Berry features early piano backing plus thumping drums which lead into a strange Latin beat. For all Berry's rock 'n' roll credentials, his is a dreary interpretation of the song which never really gets going.*

* *On the other hand The Beatles offer up a quick guitar-based intro and an altogether faster and more exciting version with John's vocal adding some much needed frenzy to the proceedings.*

This was a song that Berry claimed was "his sole doing" and he went on to say, "I take responsibility for every copy sold. I was heavy into rock 'n' roll even then and had to create something that hit the spot without question."

While that was the composer's view of his song

and his version, not everybody, it seems, agreed with him. Writing in his *Complete Guide To The Music Of The Beatles*, Robertson observed that it "took Lennon to sing this one the way it was meant to be heard" while Russell, in *The Beatles Album File & Complete Discography*, adds that "John did a better job than Chuck Berry ever did."

Bizarrely, despite it very obviously being John who took the lead vocal on the track, the New Musical Express somehow managed to get it wrong. Reviewing the album in the November 13th 1964 edition, Derek Johnson announced, "'Rock And Roll Music', the standard Chuck Berry rocker, showcases Paul in his more frenzied mood. This one's really bubbling with excitement."

While 'Rock And Roll Music' was never released as a single it did make an appearance in 1965 on the *Beatles For Sale* EP alongside 'No Reply', 'I'm A Loser' and 'Eight Days A Week' and was the title track of the 1976 Beatles double album compilation which came out following the expiry in the same year of the group's EMI recording contract..

Oddly, however, the song 'Rock And Roll Music', despite its long tenure on The Beatles live set list, was not featured in either of the famous Hollywood Bowl concerts in August 1964 and 1965 which formed the basis for the chart-topping album *The Beatles At The Hollywood Bowl*.

'Roll Over Beethoven' was another Berry song which graced The Beatles set list for many years before they finally dropped it in 1965, when only around half a dozen non-Beatle composed songs were still featured in their shows.

The Beatles put their version on their second album *With the Beatles* when George did the lead vocal work in five takes recorded in Abbey Road on the afternoon of July 30 1963. During the first couple of years when The Beatles sang the song on stage, John was lead vocalist but by 1962 George was the accepted frontman on this track, as he pointed out in the Anthology. "I sang 'Roll Over Beethoven' for *With The Beatles* – it was a song I liked. I had the Chuck Berry record and used to do it in the clubs."

Strange as it may seem, no version of 'Roll Over Beethoven' has ever graced the UK charts even though the likes of Johnny Hallyday, Status Quo and Uriah Heep did their own covers while ELO offered up an eight minute version including the opening theme to Beethoven's Fifth Symphony.

* *The original Chuck Berry version begins with a distinctive guitar solo which goes into his vocal over pounding drums. It's solo Berry all the way with no chorus and a 14 second guitar break midway, after which it speeds up to end on 2.22 seconds with five repeated title lines.*

* *Although The Beatles start out with the same guitar intro it's not quite in the Berry class and then it's George's vocal over the fuller sound of the group. Perhaps not quite as raw as the original, the foursome offer up another less than perfect guitar break before repeating the final Roll Over Beethoven five times and ending on a single guitar note at the slightly longer 2.44 seconds.*

Robertson's view in his assessment of their work was that the "Beatles sounded strangely uncomfortable the first time they cut an authentic American rock song in the studio."

Reviewing the album *With The Beatles* for *NME* in November 1963 writer Alan Smith observed, "Chuck Berry's 'Roll Over Beethoven' is an out and out rocker featuring one of George's rare vocal appearances." Meanwhile, on his original album sleeve notes the band's press officer Tony Barrow told us, "George duets with himself on this one; the boys

add to the atmosphere of active excitement by the handclapping."

The inspiration to the song, according to Berry, was his sister. "(It) was written based on the feelings I had when my sister would monopolize the piano during our youthful school years. In fact the words were aimed at Lucy instead of the maestro Ludwig van Beethoven."

In addition to its place on *With The Beatles*, 'Roll Over Beethoven' featured on the first Beatles EP released in America by Capitol Records in May 1964 – *Four By The Beatles* – alongside 'All My Loving', 'This Boy' and 'Please Mr Postman'. A version of the song recorded on August 23 1964 also appeared on the *Live Hollywood Bowl* album.

Little Richard

LITTLE RICHARD, like fellow American musician Chuck Berry, had a profound and lasting effect on The Beatles and their music. Born Richard Penniman in Macon, Georgia in 1935, he learned piano in church and from the age of 14 worked in medicine shows and vaudeville.

He began recording in 1953 and hit the R&B charts with 'Tutti Frutti' in 1955 and his 'a-wop-bom-aloo-mop-a-lop-bam-boom' opening was instantly swept into rock 'n' roll legend. Songs such as 'Lucille', 'Good Golly Miss Molly', 'Rip It Up', 'Slippin' and Slidin'', 'The Girl Can't Help It' and 'Keep A Knockin'' brought him chart success in both the US and the UK throughout the 1950s, while covers by the likes of Elvis Presley and Jerry Lee Lewis added to Richard's reputation.

In 1957 he abandoned rock 'n' roll, turned to religion and was ordained as a Seventh Day Adventist minister a year later. Eventually in 1962, with record sales in excess of 18 million to his credit, he returned to rock music and a UK tour which included sharing the bill with The Beatles.

And it was then that he realised what had been happening while he was away. Speaking in *Off The Record*, Little Richard said, "When I came back, it was shocking for me to realise how many other artists I'd influenced."

In their earliest days as The Quarrymen, the Liverpool group had regularly featured Richard's songs in their shows and, after sharing a stage in Hamburg, they appeared with him twice on October 12 1962 – on a lunch time show at the Cavern and at the Tower Ballroom, New Brighton in the evening.

Talking to Melody Maker in October 1964 Paul said, "… those early Little Richard records – those records still move me like hell", while John confirmed the singer's importance in The Beatles' Anthology. "Little Richard was one of the all-time greats. The most exciting thing about early Little Richard was when he screamed just before the solo."

Richard, it seems, was just as enthusiastic about The Beatles as he once memorably explained after seeing them live on stage during those early shared dates, "If I hadn't seen them I'd never have dreamed they were white. They have a real authentic Negro sound."

Talking years later Paul admitted how much of an influence Richard's singing style had been on him. "I did do Little Richard's voice which is a wild hoarse screaming thing, it's like an out of body experience. You have to leave your current sensibilities and go about a foot above your head to sing it."

In his autobiography,

the singer talks of teaching The Beatles' bass player his singing secret during their days in Hamburg's Star Club. "He wanted to learn my little holler so we sat at the piano going 'Oooh Oooh' til we got it." That shared experience seems to have lead to some sort of special bond growing between the American and at least one of the group. "I developed a specially close relationship with Paul McCartney but me and John couldn't make it. John had a nasty personality."

The impact Little Richard had on The Beatles didn't go unnoticed by other artists. Writing in his autobiography, Jools Holland observed, "I had always loved not only Little Richard's amazing piano playing but also his gospel shouting style of delivering a song, a big influence on The Beatles in their early days", while Sex Pistol Glen Matlock says, "I'm a sucker for that Little Richard kind of thing which Paul McCartney picked up on and did really well – you know that screaming vocal."

And one of the biggest influences in those early days was a song which remained in The Beatles' live shows for seven years – from their first shows in 1960 right through to 1966, their final year of touring – and stands as one of their greatest recording achievements.

'Long Tall Sally' was written by Richard in conjunction with Enotris Johnson and Robert 'Bumps' Blackwell and released as a single in 1956, reaching number 6 on the US pop charts, number 1 on the American R&B chart and number 3 in the UK.

According to one quote, The Beatles' version of the song stands as a tribute from Paul to one of his musical heroes. "He (Little Richard) was my idol. First song I ever sang in public was 'Long Tall Sally' at a Butlins' holiday camp talent contest when I was 14", while John once observed, "'Long Tall Sally' – when I first heard it, it was so great I couldn't speak."

Shadows rhythm guitar player Welch was a man who saw The Beatles on stage and recalls them performing this song. "'Long Tall Sally' – with Paul's sceaming Little Richard voice – always stood out. He had that raucous voice he could use on songs like this but then he could also sing a soft ballad."

The Beatles recorded the song on March 1 1964 during the sessions for the *A Hard Day's Night* album with Paul capturing the whole thing so well in one take – with Martin on piano – that no further versions were attempted.

* *Little Richard begins his original with a screaming vocal and a thumping backing band which stops intermittently as he sings the verses. His trademark scream brings in a powerful sax solo and the song closes at 2.04 seconds after five repeats of the line 'have some fun tonight'.*

* *A scream from Paul gets The Beatles' version under way and he's quickly joined by Martin's rocking piano. While the original saxophone solo is replaced by George's guitar work and there is no big band, the two versions are much the same in pace and feel and McCartney ends things just five seconds earlier with his own five repeats of the chorus line.*

John Robertson's view is that it is the "Finest rock 'n' roll performance of their career. George Harrison solo is spot on, George Martin piano thumping and Paul's throat searing vocal."

The live version of the song from the Beatles' August 23 1964 show closes the *Live At Hollywood Bowl* album, but it is best remembered as the title track to the 1964 number one UK EP which featured four tracks not previously released in the UK and is considered by many to be the greatest EP ever released.

Certainly Taylor, composer of the EP's sleeve notes, was in no doubt as to the quality of Paul's performance when he wrote, "He has never done anything better."

While Presley, Lewis,

34 From Me To You

The Kinks, Pat Boone (who bizarrely had a UK top 20 hit with the song in 1956), German heavy metal band The Scorpions and French star Johnny Hallyday all covered the track, its inclusion in the film *Backbeat* drew some criticism from Paul, the man who made the ultimate cover. "One of my annoyances about the film *Backbeat* is that they've actually taken my rock 'n' roll off me. They give John the song 'Long Tall Sally' to sing and he never sang it in his life. But now it's set in cement."

'Kansas City'/'Hey Hey Hey' combines a song by ace US writing team Jerry Leiber and Mike Stoller with Little Richard's 1959 offering which was the B-side to 'Good Golly Miss Molly'.

Leiber and Stoller originally created the track as 'K.C.Lovin'' in the early 1950s but its title was changed to 'Kansas City' by the time Wilbert Harrison hit number one in the US in 1959. The same pair wrote hits for Elvis Presley, Ben E King, The Drifters and The Coasters, but it was Richard who elected to perform 'Kansas City' as a medley with his own composition.

This was the version which The Beatles heard and copied during their live shows in 1961, 1962 and 1964 with Paul once again taking the lead vocal role. They captured it on record during their October 18 1964 session in Abbey Road and although two takes were done it was the first take, with Paul singing and Martin on piano, which was chosen for release.

* *Little Richard opens with a dour staccato guitar intro into his typical vocalising on Kansas City which runs for an even-paced 50 seconds before slipping into a faster Hey Hey Hey and an effective sax break. The whole things works up a head of steam in the second half with Richard's trademark screams and ends on a fat sax note at 2.37 seconds.*

* *The Beatles offer up much the same intro before a scream leads into George's guitar break and it runs for well over a minute before Hey Hey Hey comes into the mix. The tempo increases as Paul slips into raucous Little Richard mode and it all ends up at a shorter 2.20 seconds with Paul and the group swapping 'bye bye' chants.*

The review of the track in the November 13 1964 issue of *NME* suggests "there's ample scope for joining in on the 'hey hey hey' answering back routines" while Melody Maker are convinced that "Paul is in best blues-shouting form."

The medley was included on the group's *Beatles For Sale* album in the UK but early copies of the LP only credited the song 'Kansas City' and the writers Leiber/Stoller due to an oversight at EMI, which was rectified on later pressings to included both the title 'Hey Hey Hey' and the writer Little Richard.

In America it featured alongside a host of other cover versions on *Beatles VI* but the constant change of the original UK album track listings for the American market was something that the Beatles were not always happy about as Martin recalled, "We always objected to what the Americans did to our recordings but I had no say in it. They just did what they wanted to."

The Shirelles

THE SHIRELLES were an all-girl R&B group from New Jersey who began life as the Poguelles and ultimately rivalled the finest girl groups produced by either Phil Spector or Motown Records.

Shirley Owens, Beverley Lee, Doris Kenner and Addie Harris worked together to create a vocal style which impressed The Beatles from the early 1960s

when the songs the girls recorded began to appear in the boys' live shows.

After a decade of success throughout the sixties – during which time they notched up a trio of US top five hits but only one major UK hit – The Shirelles changed line-up, moved record labels, disbanded and re-formed throughout the 1970s and 1980s but they still claim a place in The Beatles history as the most influential girl group.

Welch, a member of The Shadows for over 50 years, agrees that The Beatles covering girl groups was not the most obvious thing to do but as he points out, "You have to remember that the audience listening to them at the time didn't know the originals – that was the clever bit."

In fact when EMI press officer Tony Barrow asked the individual Beatles to names their favourite singers way back in September 1962, The Shirelles appeared on John's list alongside the Miracles and Ben E King.

'Baby It's You' was written for the four girls by famed writer Burt Bacharach, Mack David (the brother of Bacharach's later partner Hal David) and Barney Williams and reached the US top ten in 1962, with Bacharach adding backing vocals.

On stage it was John who took the lead and he did the same job in Abbey Road on February 11 1963 when it was the penultimate song for The Beatles' first album *Please Please Me* recorded in three takes in a taxing three hour evening session.

* *The Shirelles offer a big chorus intro which drifts into a slow female lead vocal over a haunting 'sha la la' chorus. The high pitched organ break adds another dimension and the whole thing slides to halt at 2.37 seconds.*

* *The Beatles open with a tribute 'sha la la' chorus before John brings in his slightly sensitive and rasping slow vocal. George's lower pitched guitar replaces the original organ vocal and, with John singing over the chorus, it fades out at 2.32 seconds.*

In *The Beatles Album File & Complete Discography*, John Russell noted "John's ability to change the tone, pitch and feeling in his voice is finely displayed", while Jeff Robertson concluded that the performance "marked him (John) as the Beatles' most distinctive voice" in his *Complete Guide To The Music Of The Beatles*.

Back in the early 1960s the song had been one of million-selling rock singer Alice Cooper's favourite songs by the all-girl group and he was also excited by the new version. "The Beatles doing it was very, very cool"

While *Please Please Me* was The Beatles' debut UK album, the track appeared in America on their initial *Introducing …The Beatles* album released by Vee Jay, and it also made it into the charts in 1995 on a single taken from the Beatles' 1960s BBC live radio shows.

'Boys' was recorded by The Shirelles in 1961 and released as the B-side to 'Will You Still Love Me Tomorrow', the first US number one hit single by a girl group. Written by the Brill Building-based team of Luther Dixon and Wes Farrell, it was also a top five hit in the UK.

It also goes down as another song sung by two competing drummers from Liverpool. When The Beatles first included it in their live shows in 1961 it was sung by Pete Best and he held onto the role until he was replaced midway through 1962 by Ringo who carried on singing it until 1964. And he explains that taking over the vocals on the song was a natural move. "I choose 'Boys' because I also did 'Boys' when I was with Rory Storm and The Hurricanes."

Ringo did the vocal work for 'Boys' in Abbey Road on February 11 1963 and he completed the job in just one take but Paul recalls the song's lyrics posed a bit of a problem. "It was a little embarrassing because it went 'I'm talking about

boys – yeah yeah – boys' but we never thought we should call it 'Girls' just because Ringo was a boy. We just sang it the way they'd sung it."

The Shirelles open with a boogie woogie piano and the vocal comes in over the piano before the title chorus line leads into a 20 second sax break. The end, after dead on two minutes, has a fading vocal over more saxophones.

All four Beatles offer up a vocal chorus intro with guitar and drums leading into Ringo's full on solo vocal over the rest of the group's 'bop shu wop' chorus. Altogether faster and with no sax break, it gets a 22 second guitar solo from George which is introduced by Ringo, making his singing debut on record with the Beatles, urging "alright George." The version runs for 24 seconds longer than the original and features a lengthy chorus ending.

In *The Beatles Album File* Robertson suggests that Ringo sings "with enthusiasm if not subtlety" while Russell, in his *Complete Guide*, reckons he belts out lyrics "in fine form sounding like any good rock 'n' roller."

'Boys' appeared on the debut *Please Please Me* album and the American *Introducing ... The Beatles*, while the version from a show on August 23 1964 found its way on the *Live At Hollywood Bowl* album in 1977.

Arthur Alexander

ARTHUR ALEXANDER, born in 1940, hailed from Alabama and his first hit in 1961 was 'You Better Move On', a track covered by The Rolling Stones and which featured as the B-side to 'A Shot Of Rhythm And Blues', a UK hit for Johnny Kidd and The Pirates in 1963.

It was also one of a number of songs by the American singer which The Beatles introduced into their concerts – albeit for only one year – and, alongside 'Soldier Of Love 'and 'Where Have You Been All My Life', showed how much Alexander was influencing them.

"If the Beatles ever wanted a sound it was R&B. That's what we used to listen to, what we used to like and what we wanted to be like. Black, that was basically it. Arthur Alexander", was what Paul said in *The Complete Beatles Recording Sessions*, while John told Melody Maker in 1963, "On artist I like is Arthur Alexander – you don't hear much of him over here."

Confirming the group's admiration for the man who ended up as a bus driver in Cleveland before he died in 1993, George once explained, "Before going to gigs we'd meet in the record store (manager Brian Epstein's NEMS shop) after it had shut and we'd search the racks like ferrets to see what new ones there were. That's where we found artists like Arthur Alexander."

'Anna (Go To Him)' was released by Alexander in late 1962 and climbed into the US R&B top ten at about the same time as The Beatles were introducing the song into their shows with John taking the lead vocal throughout 1962 and 1963.

Confirmed by sleeve notes for The Beatles No.1 EP as "one of John's personal favourites", the track was recorded in three takes on February 11 1963, along with most of the other tracks for the *Please Please Me* album, during a frantic evening session when they taped five cover versions.

* Alexander offers up a mellow deep voice which is truly plaintive at times. With a girl chorus, strings and some clever piano work the records fades at 2.50 seconds.

* The Beatles have John's harsher and fuller voice over the rest of the group's backing chorus with a simple yet effective guitar and Ringo's

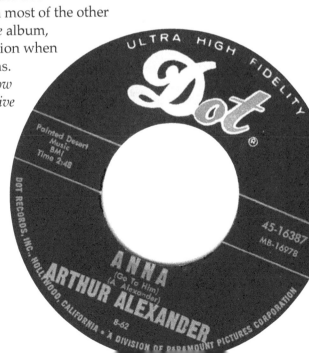

insistent beat. It closes with a simple 'go with him' on 2.54 seconds.

Robertson's assessment is that it is a "laboured cover version of an R&B hit", while Russell contends that "John's pleasing vocals do justice to the Arthur Alexander song."

According to Graham Gouldman, hearing The Beatles sing the song explained why they chose to feature it in their repertoire. "It was just a brilliant song and you can hear why they did it – it suited their voices so well."

The Cookies

THE COOKIES began their career in New York in the 1950s and after various original members left to become part of Ray Charles' group The Raelettes, Dorothy Jones, Earl-Jean McCrae and Margaret Ross became the featured line-up which worked with Ben E King and Little Eva.

In the 1960s they teamed up with the song writing team of Gerry Goffin and Carole King who worked out of New York's legendary Brill Building and wrote a string of hits for artists such as Manfred Mann, The Animals, Herman's Hermits, The Monkees and The Byrds. They gave the Cookies a US top 20 hit in 1963 with 'Don't Say Nothing (Bad About My Baby)' and in the same year another song they wrote for the Cookies was picked up on by The Beatles.

'Chains' reached the UK top 50 and hit the US top 20 and during 1963 briefly became part of The Beatles' live set – probably more as a tribute to the composers Goffin and King than to the girl group.

Recorded in Abbey Road during the frenetic Febuary 11 1963 session that finished off the *Please Please Me* album, the song was over in four takes with John Paul and George sharing the vocal duties.

* The Cookies offer their all female chorus alongside intermittent sax breaks before a solo voice takes two verses in between repeated choruses. It all

finishes on 2.30 seconds with a fade out of repeated 'chains of love.'

* The Beatles begin with John's harmonica intro before John Paul and George get together to share a more earthy vocal – with George taking a brief husky solo spot – and it runs out with a similar faded 'chains of love' at 2.23 seconds.

For John Robertson it is a "charming cheerful cover", while Beatles' PR man Tony Barrow's notes on The Beatles *No. 1* EP say of the final track, "'Chains' is (or are!) used to bind together the voice of George, John and Paul in a hard hitting finale."

Dr Feelgood

DR FEELGOOD was in fact US bluesman William Lee Perryman who performed under the name Piano Red and then created Dr Feelgood & the Interns to record the song Dr Feelgood in 1962. However it was B-side of that minor US hit which captured the attention of The Beatles.

'Mr Moonlight' was written by Roy Lee Johnson and became a feature of The Beatles' shows in 1962 and 1963 when John took the lead as he did in the studio on August 14 1964, when four takes were completed, and again on October 18 when it was done in three more takes and Paul's Hammond organ was added.

* Dr Feelgood start with a chopping beat over layered vocals and an understated lead

voice. It starts to get laboured and leads into a short simple Latin style guitar break, and a series of repeated titles ends it all on 2.26 seconds.

* The Beatles begin with John belting out the title at the outset before the similar choppy beat comes in. John's singing is altogether better and more effective than the original and is accompanied by group harmonies and Paul's dramatic Hammond organ before ending on repeated titles at a slightly longer 2.33 seconds.

While Roberston declares that it is a "bizarre mediocre version of another song from black America", Melody Maker's review of *Beatles For Sale* in October 1964 concluded that it was "the only one which does not make immediate appeal."

At the same time the *NME* of November 13 1964 reckoned, "'Mr Moonlight' is perhaps the most ear-catching track on the LP. It has a predominantly earthy sound with John blues shouting in passages with forceful and raucous ensemble vocalising off setting his solo."

The song, a favourite on the Northern beat circuit in the 1960s, was also recorded by The Hollies and The Merseybeats who featured it as the B-side of their biggest hit 'I Think Of You' but titled it 'Mister Moonlight' and bizarrely failed to credit the writer.

The Donays

THE DONAYS were one of the many girl groups which emerged in the US in the early 1960s but their career was both short and not very sweet as it seems that they recorded only one record for an obscure label called Correc-tone.

Formed in Detroit and led by Yvonne Allen, who later joined the Motown group The Elgins, the Donays' sole recording, which some suggest featured the Motown house musicians, somehow found its way onto The Beatles wavelength along with the other tracks originally recorded by girl groups.

"They just picked up great songs and didn't worry about who had sung it originally", says Gouldman. "It didn't seem to matter to them whether it was boys or girls." .

'Devil In His (Her) Heart' was written by singer Ricky Dee under his real name of Richard Drapkin and recorded by The Donays in 1962 under its original title 'Devil In His Heart'.

Somewhere along the line it came to the attention of The Beatles who put the song into their shows in 1962 and 1963 when, as George took the lead and to avoid any embarrassment, it was re-titled 'Devil In Her Heart'. On July 18 1963 it was completed in Abbey Road in just three takes with Ringo on maracas.

* The Donays start with piano into a high pitched chorus before Allen's solo voice moves in to take the song through at a slowish pace with the focus on single voice and a simple guitar backing through to a fade out at 2.32 seconds.

* The Beatles replace the original piano with a guitar intro and George's lighter less soulful vocal. After a building chorus, the tempo picks up and the Beatles end the whole thing ends abruptly on 2.25 seconds.

Talking years later George offered some insight into where The Beatles found this and other songs. "'Devil In Her Heart' and 'Money' were songs that we'd picked up and played in the store (the NEMS shop in Liverpool) and thought were interesting."

Buddy Holly

BUDDY HOLLY was born Charles Hardin Holley

in Lubbock, Texas in 1936 and first found fame as half of the duo Buddy and Bob which supported both Bill Haley and Elvis Presley. After forming Buddy Holly and the Two Tones, he emerged as Buddy Holly and The Crickets in 1957 with independent producer and writer Norman Petty in close attendance.

In the two years before his death in a plane crash in February 1959, Holly charted in both the US and the UK with a host of records including 'Peggy Sue', 'That'll Be The Day', 'Oh Boy', 'Rave On', 'Maybe Baby', 'It's So Easy' and 'It Doesn't Matter Anymore' and most of them ended up in early Beatles' shows.

His influence on The Beatles was such that the band took their name from his group the Crickets, but there was something else that inspired them as Paul once explained. "John and I started to write because of Buddy Holly. It was like Wow! He writes and is a musician."

John too was moved by the man from Texas. "Buddy Holly was great and he wore glasses which I liked. He was the first one we were really aware of in England who could play and sing at the same time." He also admitted that after initially wanting to be like the song writing team of Goffin and King, he and Paul aspired to be like Holly. Talking to Melody Maker in February 1963 he said, "It's true we've written about 100 songs – some of them are rubbish of course. We started in the Buddy Holly days when everyone thought they could turnout simple songs like his and we've been writing ever since."

While Holly's 'That'll Be The Day' was apparently the first song John ever learnt to play on a guitar, it was Paul who actually saw him perform during his 25 date UK tour in 1958 and later admitted, "I love Buddy Holly. I've been crazy about him since I was a kid." So crazy in fact that in 1976 he bought the rights to Holly's song catalogue, thanks to the efforts of his then father in law. "Lee (Eastman) got on to the man who owned Buddy Holly's stuff and bought that for me."

Later he also became the owner of the cufflinks Holly was wearing when he died – they were given to him by Petty – but despite Holly's huge influence on The Beatles they only ever officially recorded one of his songs.

'Words of Love' was recorded by Holly in 1957 and became a minor hit for The Diamonds, reaching number 13 in the US chart in the same year. It first featured in Quarrymen performances in 1957 and became a regular in Beatle shows between 1960 and 1962 with John and George duetting.

However, by the time they came to record the song in Abbey Road on October 18 1964, the vocals had switched to John and Paul who completed the song in three takes, as (according to Derek Taylor's album sleeve notes) "Ringo plays a packing case", at the end of an afternoon/evening session recording tracks for the Beatles For Sale album.

* *Buddy Holly starts with a typically light intro which leads into a lower register vocal. All done at a slow pace with hmmmms to the fore throughout and after a simple Holly guitar break it's all over in just 1.50 seconds.*

* *The Beatles begin with same style intro but the whole thing gets a fuller feel through the close harmony vocals of John and Paul including Holly's trademarks hmmmms. George's guitar break leads into an extended second half to the song with hmmm/aaaaah choruses taking it to just over two minutes.*

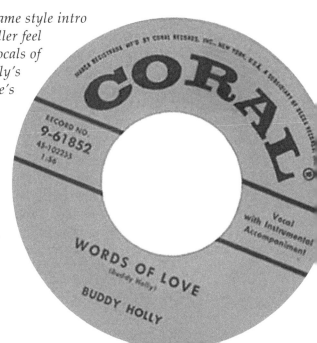

Russell suggests that 'Words Of Love' is the "best example of how John and Paul blended their voices" while Glen Matlock is less impressed and admits, "I put this in the slushy file ... Holly was always a bit geeky for me."

NME's reviewer Derek Johnson wrote in November 1964, "I found it particularly outstanding for George's attractive guitar figure and Ringo's conga drum" while MM writer Chris Welch simply said that the track "bowed in the direction of Buddy Holly."

The Isley Brothers

THE ISLEY BROTHERS hailed from Cincinnati where Rudolph, Ronald, O'Kelly and Vernon Isley began singing in a local church but, following Vernon's death in a road accident, the remaining three brothers travelled to New York in search of a record deal.

After spells with RCA – where 'Shout' (later a major hit for Lulu) made the US top 50 – and Atlantic, they linked up with Wand and producer Bert Berns who steered their career until they set up their own T-Neck label.

They included the late Jimi Hendrix in their touring band before joining forces with Motown and hitting the UK top ten with 'This Old Heart Of Mine' and 'Behind A Painted Smile'. With the addition of brothers Ernie and Marvin and cousin Chris Jasper, the extended Isley Brothers found new success in the 1970s with 'That Lady', 'Highways Of My Mind', 'Summer Breeze' and 'Harvest For The World' before the group split up in 1984.

But it was one song from the original Isley Brothers trio which still stands out today as a Beatles classic.

'Twist And Shout' was credited to the song writing team of Bert Russell – who was in fact named Berns – and Phil Medley (who it seems might also have been Berns) and first recorded by the Isley Brothers in 1962 when it reached both the US and UK pop charts and peaked at number 2 on the American R&B chart.

Bizarrely the original recording of the songs was done by a group called The Top Notes and was produced by Phil Spector who would later play a significant part in the acrimonious splitting up of The Beatles in 1970.

Almost as soon as The Isley's version was released, The Beatles included the song in their live shows where it stayed until 1965, becoming a classic John show-stopper, although performing it live did occasionally pose a problem, as he once recounted. "I hate singing 'Twist And Shout' when there's a coloured artist on the bill. It doesn't seem right you know. It seems to be their music and I feel sort of embarrassed. Makes me curl up … they can do these songs much better than us."

However, talking to Melody Maker in February 1963, John spoke fondly of the song. "One number we do is 'Twist And Shout'. That's a knockout number but I don't know whether you'd call it rhythm and blues."

The Beatles' legendary version of the song was recorded on February 11 1963 at the end of a day when they recorded the 12 songs that would appear on their debut *Please Please Me* album alongside the title track single and its B-side 'Ask Me Why'.

At around 10pm there was just one song to be done and John set about recording 'Twist And Shout' in just one take with (so the story goes) the help of a throat lozenge and a glass of milk and the result, according to John Robertson, was "Britain's best rock 'n' roll record to date."

The Isleys offer a soft,

controlled soulful vocal over a chorus which leads into a brass backing and instrumental break. The familiar rising 'aaaaaaaaah' chorus goes into a slightly half-hearted scream and ends up at 2.25 seconds on a sole falsetto voice.

* The Beatles come in with a chunky group intro and John's harsh vocal which gets more and more strained and stretched as it goes on. Repeated guitar and drum breaks lead the build-up into the chorus of aaaaaaaahs, a spine-tingling John scream and his almost spent pay-off vocal on 2.30 seconds.

Producer George Martin recalled in his autobiography *All You Need Is Ears*, "'Twist And Shout' had to be right on the first take because I knew perfectly well that if we had to do it a second time it would never be as good."

The track signed off the group's debut album and was also the title track of their first ever EP which sold over 800,000 copies and reached number 2 on the UK singles chart. It also peaked at number two in the US where it was released as a single in March 1964.

While rival sixties group Brian Poole and The Tremeloes hit number four with their version in 1963, it was The Beatles cover of The Isley classic which influenced one young man. "The very first record I bought out of my pocket money when I was about eight or nine was 'Twist And Shout'", says former Sex Pistol Glen Matlock. "That's when I got into the Beatles and Lennon's vocal is one of the all-time classic performances."

Peggy Lee

PEGGY LEE, born Norma Egstrom in North Dakota in 1920, was a noted jazz singer who worked with the likes of Benny Goodman, Duke Ellington and Quincy Jones and was signed to both Decca and Capitol. Among her collection of hit records were classics such as 'The

Lady Is A Tramp', 'Mr Wonderful', 'Fever' and 'Is That All There Is?', but it was her version of a particular show tune which inspired The Beatles.

'Till There Was You' was written by Meredith Wilson for the Broadway musical *The Music Man* before Lee recorded it in 1961 when it reached the UK top 30. It was featured in The Beatles' live shows between 1961 and 1964 and was another song that was part of the group's audition for Decca in 1962.

Paul was introduced to Lee's singing by a cousin and he recalled the moment in the book *Yesterday & Today*. "So eventually I went out and bought a few Peggy Lee records and 'Till There Was You' was among them. I had no idea until much later that it was from *The Music Man*. I don't think I'd have done it if I'd known that. There would have been too much stigma in our world. A show tune! Are you kidding?"

The fact that it was a show tune also came as a surprise to Bruce Welch. "It was a song we all thought they had written and nobody realised it came from a musical. It was a great ballad and they would have done it because they considered it to be a great song."

According to Paul, including the song on stage "showed we weren't just another rock 'n' roll band", and he went further to explain, "I could pull out 'Till There Was You' – the more cabaret things."

The band began recording it, with Paul obviously on lead vocal, in Abbey Road on July 18, 1963 but they were unhappy with the first

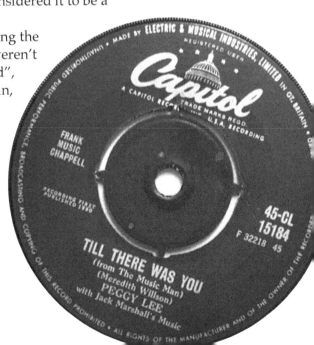

three takes and returned to it on July 30 when, with Ringo on bongos instead of drums, they finished it in a further five takes.

*   *Peggy Lee puts a distinctive slightly sweet jazzy vocal intro over the piano and full orchestra backing. It is sung at a slow-ish tempo with an at times breathy vocal and the whole thing moves into a Latin rhythm near the end.*

*   *The Beatles continue the Latin feel with a simple guitar and bongos intro which leads into Paul's fuller and less saccharin vocalising. After a guitar break midway, the song ends with a twice repeated title and a single guitar note.*

According to Robertson it was sung as if Paul "meant every word of it and George Harrison contributed an accomplished acoustic guitar solo", while *NME*'s Alan Smith, reviewing *With The Beatles* in the November 15 1963 issue, wrote, "While most of the album is wild and up-tempo, the Peggy Lee hit 'Till There Was You' is a distinctive contrast."

Interestingly the publishing rights to 'Till There Was You' and the *The Music Man* soundtrack were acquired by Paul McCartney and they sit within his MPL operation alongside the rights to music from *Annie*, *Chorus Line*, *Grease* and *Guys & Dolls*.

The Marvelettes

THE MARVELETTES came from Detroit, Michigan and featured Gladys Horton, Wanda Young, Katherine Anderson, Juanita Cowart and Georgina Dobbins. They started out in 1961 as high school group the Casinyets before becoming The Marvels and signing to Motown where Berry Gordy re-named them The Marvelettes.

During the 1960s the group, who lost Cowart and Dobbins early on, notched up 23 US Hot 100 hits including the Motown label's first ever American chart topper. And, despite working with the likes of (Brian)

Holland (Lamont) Dozier (Eddie) Holland and Smokey Robinson they only managed one UK hit ('When You're Young And In Love' in 1967) but it was their first US hit which inspired the Beatles.

'Please Mr Postman' was a million-seller which took 15 weeks to reach number one in America in 1961 which was when The Beatles first put it into their set list, where it stayed for the next two years. It was written by group member Dobbins along with Brian Holland, Robert Bateman and William Garrett and the original recording featured a young Marvin Gaye on drums.

John took the lead on The Beatles' version both on stage and in Abbey Road studios on July 30 1963 when they recorded it in nine takes with some overdubbing to get it right.

* The Marvelettes open with percussion over the girls before lead singer Horton takes over with a soulful solo. Piano comes in and the vocal gets a little harsher over some annoying chirping backing vocals with drums still to the front. It fades over the 'wait a minute, wait a minute' chorus at 2.24 seconds.

* The Beatles offer a fuller group intro with strong percussion into an altogether bigger sound with John's vocal leading the rest of the group. He forces the song along over a more impressive backing chorus and puts greater emphasis on the lyrics until the same repeated chorus fades out at 2.34 seconds.

Beatles' author John Robertson is of the view that "Lennon's performance was so magical it made the original sound like an imitation", while Alice Cooper describes 'Please Mr Postman' as simply "a great, great Beatles record."

Buck Owens

BUCK OWENS was a superstar country singer who was born Alvis Owens in Texas in 1929 and learned mandolin and guitar as a child in Arizona. He moved to Bakersfield in California and worked as a session player before creating the Buckaroos and notching up a host of country hits and winning the Country Music Award as Best Band.

He recorded and toured with Emmylou Harris and Dwight Yoakham and his management and music publishing companies – plus studio and radio stations – led to his adopted town being known as Buckersfield, but it was a song he recorded in 1963 which brought him to the attention of The Beatles.

'Act Naturally' was written by Johnny Russell and Voni Morison, became a US country number one hit for Owens and was a favourite of Beatles' drummer Ringo who was always the group's biggest country music fan. It was included in live shows in 1965 only and in the same year, on June 17, it was recorded at Abbey Road.

The group had rejected the song 'If You've Got Trouble' as Ringo's solo for the *Help!* album and this song was chosen as the replacement track. It was recorded in 13 takes which included Paul's Americanised backing vocals with Ringo only adding his vocal on the last take.

* *Owens starts off in slow country mode with his twanging guitar and a country drawl to the fore. With a double tracked vocal chorus, the song runs for 2.17 seconds.*

* *The Beatles version features Ringo's lighter and less country-influenced vocal and a faster tempo. George brings in some country guitar while Ringo keeps up the beat and it all ends at slightly longer 2.27 seconds with a brief guitar solo.*

Later Ringo confirmed that the song was his choice. "I found it on a Buck Owens record and I said 'This is the one I am going to be doing and they said OK'." What he didn't know was that his performance would be the last complete cover version The Beatles recorded as part of an official studio album.

While *MM* noted in their July 1965 review of the soundtrack album from the band's second movie that it was "the only song that sounds as though it comes from a film", *NME* said, "'Act Naturally' is Ringo's solitary showcase … it's a perfect novelty vehicle for him."

In addition to *Help!*, the song also appeared on America's *Yesterday … And Today* album plus the UK EP *Yesterday* and it also found a huge audience as the B-side of the US number one single 'Yesterday'. Ringo sang the song on the Ed Sullivan Show in 1965 and also recorded a version with Buck Owens in Abbey Road in 1989, which reached the US country chart top 30. He later recorded another version with his Ringo All Stars band.

Smokey Robinson

SMOKEY ROBINSON was born William Robinson in Detroit in 1940 and, as singer with the Miracles, was among the first artists to be signed to the fledgling Motown Records.

Their record 'Shop Around' was the label's first pop hit in 1960 and Robinson not only starred as vocalist on major US and UK hits such as 'Tears Of A Clown', 'Tracks Of My Tears', 'I Second That Emotion' and 'Being With You', but also produced and wrote hits for Motown acts including Mary Wells, The Temptations, Marvin

54 From Me To You

Gaye, The Four Tops and The Supremes.

The music of Motown that came out of Detroit and drifted into the UK in the early 1960s had an immediate impact on The Beatles as Ringo pointed out. "We all had The Miracles (records) and we all had Barrett Strong and people like that", while Paul also confirmed the importance of the leader of the Miracles. "The Miracles were a big influence on us where Little Richard had been earlier. Now (around 1964/65) for us Motown artists were taking the place of Richard. Smokey Robinson was like God in our eyes."

Even so the Beatles only ever featured one Robinson song in either their live shows or on record.

'You Really Got A Hold On Me' was a US million seller which reached number two in the US pop chart in 1962, topped the American R&B chart but still failed to register in the UK. However The Beatles still chose to include it in their live shows throughout 1962 and 1963, with John taking the lead, and also to record it for their second album *With The Beatles* during an Abbey Road session on July 18 1963.

On that first day of recording for the new album, they completed 11 takes of the song with Martin accompanying John's vocal on piano. A further four track version was recorded on October 18 but the final version came from the earlier takes.

* Robinson starts with a simple piano and guitar intro which extends into his slow vocal before the Miracles chime in and repeat his lines. His trademark falsetto vocal is featured ahead of a brass break which takes the song almost to a full stop before it picks up to run out at 2.56 seconds with piano and guitar behind the title line.

* The Beatles opt for a fuller piano and guitar intro which leads into John over the group's chorus work. Even though his vocal is lower as he strains for the high notes, John still imparts real feeling into the song over deft guitar and piano work. Moving along more as a rock ballad than a soul song, it runs out with an instrumental part at three minutes making it the longest Beatles record to date.

Jeff Russell points out that the "lead vocal is brilliantly handled by John", while John Robertson goes a step further and suggests that the original is "easily outclassed by The Beatles effortless interpretation."

For Paul, the fact that the group could do songs like this was one of the things that made them special. "That was a great aspect of us. John could do something like 'A Shot Of Rhythm And Blues'or 'You Really Got A Hold On Me' – you could call that cool."

The Beatles did record the song again in their own Savile Row studio on January 26 1969 as part of the aborted *Get Back* album project. It was included in an unreleased medley of songs alongside 'Shake Rattle And Roll', 'Blue Suede Shoes', 'Kansas City', 'Miss Ann', and 'Lawdy Miss Clawdy' which never saw the light of day, although the first two tracks – plus 'Rip It Up' – appeared on Volume 3 of The Beatles *Anthology* released in 1996.

Barrett Strong

BARRETT STRONG, born in Mississippi in 1941, has the distinction of notching up Motown's first ever hit record in 1960 with a song which The Beatles included in their live shows and on their second album.

After his early success as a singer, Strong moved on to forge a celebrated and successful song writing and production career in partnership with Norman Whitfield. Working in the

56 From Me To You

Detroit headquarters of Motown, they were responsible for hits such as 'Papa Was A Rolling Stone', 'Cloud Nine', 'Can't Get Next To You', 'Just My Imagination' and 'I Heard It Through The Grapevine'.

The new-found influence of black American pop music in The Beatles' songbook was quickly spotted by producer Martin who commented "They certainly knew more about Motown and black music than anybody else did and that was a tremendous influence on them."

Talking to Rolling Stone founder and editor Jan Wenner, John Lennon confirmed the group's fascination with one particular sort of music coming out of America. "It was the black music we dug. We felt we had the message which was 'listen to this music'. It was the same in Liverpool; we felt very exclusive and underground in Liverpool listening to Barrett Strong and all those old time records."

'Money (That's What I Want)' came from the pen of Motown founder Berry Gordy and Janie Bradford and it earned Strong a debut number 23 hit on the US pop chart – and the number 2 spot on the US R&B chart – in 1960, but it was not a hit in the UK until sixties group Bern Elliott & The Fenman reached number 14 in 1963.

The Beatles adopted 'Money' as part of their live shows in the same year as the record came out in America and included it until 1964. It was also one of the songs they performed in their unsuccessful audition for Decca Records on January 1 1962 and then, as was always the case, John took the lead vocal.

It was recorded by the band on July 18 1963 on the first day of recording for their follow-up album to *Please Please Me* – which they had released just four months earlier – and completed in seven takes.

* Barrett Strong has a pounding piano/percussion intro into his pleading vocal. The title is much repeated along with the chorus line 'that's what I want' and after a guitar/ drum/bass break, it returns to the same title/chorus mix through to a fade out at 2.34 seconds.

* The Beatles opt for the same piano/drum intro before John's vocal comes in at much the same tempo as the original but wilder and less controlled

than Strong's offering. A similar instrumental break leads into the familiar combination of title line and chorus through to a single note ending on 2.46 seconds.

The Beatles' offering certainly impressed Sex Pistol's bassman Matlock who says simply, "I think their version of 'Money' is great", while Robertson goes further to suggest that the "original version is knocked off the pavement by Lennon's steamroller vocal."

In addition to featuring as the closing track on *With The Beatles*, 'Money' popped up on the 1963 *All My Loving* EP and the American *The Beatles Second Album* release, while John featured the track on his 1969 *Live Peace In Toronto* album.

Gene Vincent

GENE VINCENT was born Gene Craddock in 1935 in the US coastal town of Norfolk in Virginia. He left the navy after breaking his leg in a motor cycle accident and turned to music after meeting local disc jockey Bill Davis who helped him make his first record – 'Be-Bop-A-Lula' – and took over his management.

After signing to Capitol Records in 1956, Vincent formed the Blue Caps (named after US President Eisenhower's favourite golf cap), with Cliff Gallup, Willie Williams, Jack Neal and Dickie Harrell.

His appearance in the film *The Girl Can't Help It*

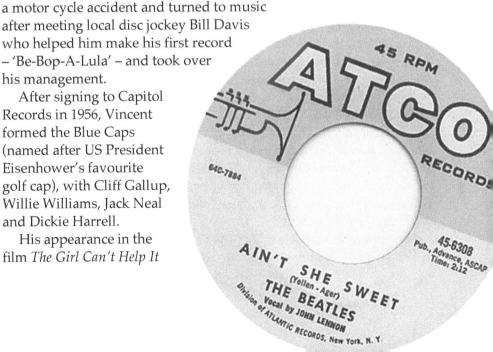

brought him to the attention of The Beatles – who he later appeared with at The Cavern in Liverpool and in the Star Club in Hamburg – and turned their attention towards the 1927 roarin' twenties song written by Jack Yeller and Milton Ager.

'Ain't That A Shame' was first recorded by the New York Syncopators followed by the likes of Pearl Bailey, Eddie Cantor, Frankie Lymon and Frank Sinatra while Vincent elected to include it on his first album, the US number 16 hit *Blue Jean Bop*.

Despite taking the view, according to Paul, that the song had "cred" because it was on a Gene Vincent album, The Beatles were forced to change how they performed the song live. "Gene Vincent's recording is very mellow and high-pitched and I used to do it like that", said John. But the Germans said 'harder harder' – they all wanted it a bit more like a march – so we ended up doing a harder version."

They took that 'harder' style into the studio with them when they got the chance to record in a professional studio in Hamburg under the watchful eyes of German producer (and band leader) Bert Kaempfert – the man who wrote the original version of Elvis Presley's hit 'Wooden Heart'.

* Gene Vincent accompanied by his Blue Cats offers up a slow paced version featuring a falsetto almost eerie lead vocal which features extended words and some Buddy Holly-style hiccupping. Guitarist Cliff Gallup's guitar break is a strong and effective interlude and the song ends after 2.27 seconds on his guitar notes.

* By comparison The Beatles offer the lead to John who goes into the raucous louder or 'harder' vocal style later associated with 'Twist & Shout'. Their version goes along at a faster pace, almost chugging along, but George's guitar break is weak and inauspicious compared to Gallup's. This version closes at 2.10 seconds and ends with John repeating the chorus "I ask you very confidentially ...."

The general consensus is that The Beatles (also known in Germany in 1961 as The Beat Boys) went into the studio in June 1961 to back singer Tony Sheridan who they had also accompanied on stage. He was signed to the German label Polydor and, with Pete Best on drums, The Beatles recorded 'My Bonnie', 'The Saints', 'Why' and 'Nobody's Child'.

Perhaps as some sort of favour, The Beatles were then allowed to use the last hour of the session to record a couple of numbers without Sheridan. They chose 'Ain't She Sweet' and an instrumental written by John and George called 'Cry For A Shadow' but still failed, according to George, to get the appropriate recognition. "Although we did 'Ain't She Sweet' and 'Cry For A Shadow' without Sheridan they didn't even put our name on the record. That's why it's so pathetic that later, when we'd become famous, they put the record out as The Beatles With Tony Sheridan."

Writing about Vincent, Colin Larkin in his *Encyclopedia of Rock* (Muze 1998), said that "… his tender version of 'Ain't She Sweet' demonstrated his potential as an all round entertainer" while Ian McDonald – in his book *Revolution In The Head* (Fourth Estate 1994) queried The Beatles decision to record the song at all. "While it presumably went down well with the raucous clientele of the Top Ten Club, it made little sense as a choice for The Beatles' first professional recording and fails to reward attention in hindsight."

Issued in 1964 on Polydor, The Beatles' version of 'Ain't She Sweet' reached number 29 in the UK and was also featured on an album released by the American Atco label in 1964 entitled *Ain't She Sweet* where it featured an

overdubbed drum track from Pretty Purdie as the US record company weren't happy with Best's efforts on the original. The album also included three songs by Sheridan and eight cover versions by US group The Swallows.

The original Hamburg recording was included on The Beatles' *Anthology 1* release while a newer version was featured on *Anthology 3*. Recorded on July 24 1969, before their group's Abbey Road sessions, it features 'Ain't She Sweet' – done in the mellower style of Vincent's original – as part of an impromptu Gene Vincent-jam including 'Be-Bop-A-Lula' and 'Who Slapped John?'.

A survivor of the April 1960 car crash in which Eddie Cochran was killed, Vincent appeared on the same bill as John Lennon's Plastic Ono Band at the Toronto Rock'n'Roll Revival – alongside Chuck Berry, Jerry Lee Lewis and Little Richard in 1969 – but died in October 1971 aged just 36.

Lenny Welch

LENNY WELCH'S main claim to fame is as the singer who had a minor hit in 1962 with a song composed originally as an instrumental for a Broadway stage play. His version was also the one which probably inspired The Beatles to adopt the song as part of their stage show in 1962 and 1963.

'A Taste Of Honey' was written by Bobby Scott as the incidental music to a play which was later filmed in the UK. In 1962 it won a Grammy as Best Instrumental Theme and it also won favour with The Beatles after Ric Marlow added lyrics and Welch recorded it.

Paul took the lead vocals on a song that he confirmed was "one of my big numbers in Hamburg – a bit of a ballad. It was different but it used to get requested a lot." He also claimed that performing this sort of song in the early days was important for the band because "when we did get to the level of the Ed Sullivan show, we were real and not just some little schmucks from out of town."

Another of the songs recorded during the *Please Please Me* session on February 11 1963, it was completed in seven takes in the afternoon with Paul double tracking his vocal.

* *Welch opens with a female chorus and moves into his slow sweet vocal over a simple strummed guitar. Alternate boy/girl choruses take it through to Welch's vocal and chorus with a faded ending at 2.36 seconds.*

* *The Beatles pitch in with a full group opening chorus before Paul brings in his more plaintive and less saccharine vocal. The whole thing has a much fuller feel and moves along at a faster pace leading to a slow fade over lead vocal and chorus after just two minutes.*

Included on *Please Please Me*, it also featured on the Vee Jay label's *Introducing ... The Beatles* album in America and on the UK EP *Twist And Shout* where Barrow's sleeve notes suggest that Paul's is a "sad, slightly nostalgic version" before concluding that his performance is "a haunting piece of atmosphere balladeering."

While a host of other acts – including Trini Lopez, Acker Bilk, Barbra Streisand and Tony Bennett – have all recorded the song it was a version by Herb Alpert, with Leon Russell on piano, which won the song its second Grammy when it was voted Best Record in 1965 – beating the classic Paul McCartney song 'Yesterday' along the way.

62 From Me To You

PS...

'<u>Maggie May (Mae)</u>' has a unique place in the history of The Beatles' recording career as the last piece of music not written by any of the group to appear on a Beatles' studio album.

It is a traditional Liverpool folk song about a local prostitute from the city's notorious Lime Street district who once robbed a sailor. She became something of a legend in the city and was the subject of a musical by respected local writer Alun Owen, who also wrote the screenplay for *A Hard Day's Night*. The song was part of early Quarrymen shows in the 1950s and was recorded by The Vipers Skiffle Group, featuring TV/radio presenter Wally Whyton, but was banned by the BBC because of its 'sexy' lyrics. The Beatles seemingly used it as a warm-up track before and during recording sessions.

They recorded a short 38 second send-up version with John leading the way in an accentuated 'Scouse' accent in their Savile Row studios on January 24 1969. It was thrown in between takes of' On Our way Home' – later re-titled 'Two Of Us' – and finally appeared in the middle of the *Let It Be* album with a composers' credit that read "Trad arr Lennon/McCartney/Harrison/Starkey."

Covers from the live set list

The songs featured in this section were at the very heart of the live shows performed by The Beatles in their earliest years as they pounded away in sweaty, smoky, dingy and dirty clubs and halls. It wasn't a glamorous journey but a necessary one which was perfectly summed up by George Harrison when he said, "We had to learn millions of songs. We had to play so long we just played everything."

The Beatles – as The Beatles – toured and played live around the world for seven years starting in 1960 with a line up that featured John Lennon, Paul McCartney,

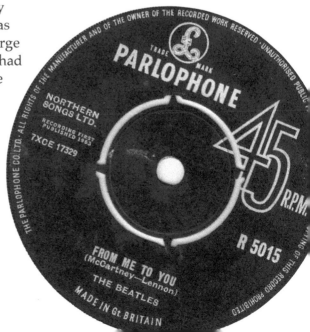

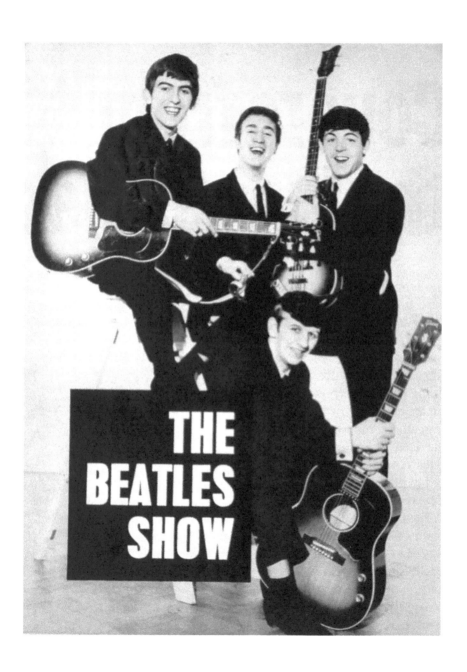

George Harrison, Stuart Sutcliffe and a couple of stand-in drummers until Pete Best took his seat behind the four guitarists in August 1960.

During the final three years of their existence as a touring band, with Ringo Starr on drums, The Beatles' shows grew shorter and shorter, compared to the lengthy sessions in Hamburg nightclubs and gigs in and around Liverpool, and also included fewer and fewer covers as they focussed on the songs written by Lennon and McCartney.

But while they did continue to feature songs written by other composers – mainly those that they had recorded and included on their albums – they only ever included in their live performances one number written by fellow group member Harrison … 'If I Needed Someone' featured in concerts in 1966, the year they stopped touring.

Many of the non-Lennon/McCartney songs played live by The Beatles are already featured in the previous chapter as they were the ones the 'fab four' deemed to be worth recording and including on a Beatles album, EP or single.

Now we move on to a collection of compositions which have a place in The Beatles' story because they played a major part in the group's learning curve, its development and eventual emergence as a fully fledged pop group of the highest calibre.

Records show that the following 31 songs were included in Beatles' shows for at least three years from 1960 but never made it in to the studio and on to an official Beatles' record. Many of them (17 in fact) were featured on the 1994 album *The Beatles Live At The BBC* which brought together their performances

on shows such as *Pop Go The Beatles, Saturday Club* and *Top Gear* while a further four versions made it on to The Beatles *Anthology 1* album from 1995 which means that 10 of the songs performed regularly by The Beatles over three years have never made it on to any official vinyl or CD release but exist only on bootlegs or audition tapes.

As it would have been an original or popular version of these songs – recorded and released in the late 1950s or even early 1960s – which the group heard on the radio, on a friend's record player or in their local clubs and coffee bars, they are being listed alphabetically by artist (placed in order according to the number of songs they supplied to Beatles' shows over the years) rather than by songwriter – although in some cases they are one and the same.

In 1960 The Beatles performed a combined total of over 100 songs in their live shows, by 1963 the total was less than 40 and in 1966 their set list came from just 12 songs – nine by Lennon-McCartney, one by Harrison and two perennial covers … 'Long Tall Sally' and 'Rock And Roll Music'. The majority of the songs listed here were all part of Beatles' performances in 1960, 1961 and 1962 while one was featured from 1961 through to 1963 and another – the notable exception – which was included for a record four years from 1960 until 1963.

While many famous titles made up part of The Beatles' repertoire for just two years only to disappear without trace – including classics such as 'Blue Suede Shoes', 'Hound Dog', 'Lawdy Miss Clawdy', 'Peggy Sue', 'Short Fat Fanny', 'Whole Lotta Shakin'' and 'Bony Moronie' – the following songs would seem to be the ones The Beatles enjoyed listening to, liked performing and wanted their fans to hear.

Carol

'Carol' was written by one of The Beatles' all-time favourite performers and composers, Chuck Berry. By the time 'Carol' was released in August 1958 on Chess Records, Berry had had a run of five US top ten hits and a couple of UK top 30 entries and was firmly established as a major influence on The Beatles.

While Carol was a number 18 hit in America it failed to make an impression on the British charts but The Beatles featured it – with John as lead vocalist – as a regular in their concerts from 1960 until 1962. It eventually made it on to *Live At The BBC* album and also appeared on The Rolling Stones debut album in 1964 and has been covered by the likes of The Doors, Status Quo and Tom Petty.

Johnny B. Goode

'Johnny B. Goode' was recorded and released by Berry in April 1958 and almost immediately became part of The Beatles' repertoire when they toured as Johnny and The Moondogs and the Silver Beetles. And they continued to perform it, with John taking the lead, through until 1962. It was John who admitted that "Chuck Berry was a huge influence on me with 'Johnny B. Goode'" before adding that these two songs were part of his musical schooling. "I learned the solos on 'Johnny B. Goode' and 'Carol'." And Paul agreed, citing Berry as "a huge influence with 'Johnny B. Goode'."

The song was a major top ten hit in the US for Berry when it was issued

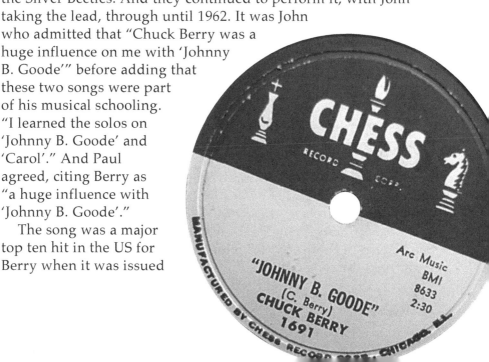

EUROPE'S MOST LUXURIOUS THEATRE **ABC BLACKPOOL** PHONE 24233

on the Chess label with 'Around And Around' as the B-side. Considered to be a fictionalised version of his own life, Berry changed the original line "poor colored boy who played guitar" to "poor country boy" in order to get radio play in the States.

Voted one of the 500 songs that inspired rock 'n' roll according to the American Rock 'n' Roll Hall of Fame, 'Johnny B. Goode' was one of a trio of songs by Berry – alongside 'Bye Bye Johnny' and 'Go Go Go' – which featured 'Johnny' – and appealed to a host of artists alongside The Beatles (who added a 1964 Saturday Club recording to *Live At The BBC*) including Buck Owens, Judas Priest, Peter Tosh, The Beach Boys, Jimi Hendrix and the Sex Pistols. In February 1972 John Lennon and Chuck Berry performed the song on US TV on The Mike Douglas Show.

Little Queenie

Little Queenie holds a unique place in Beatles history. The Chuck Berry song written in 1959 has the distinction of being featured regularly in Beatles' live shows for four years from 1960 but never ever being officially recorded by the band.

The fact that they performed the song throughout their years in Hamburg led to 'Little Queenie' eventually appearing on various bootleg recordings made at the famous Star Club but it was always odd that a number that they obviously enjoyed playing live never appeared on any of their albums.

Berry's original recording was the B-side of his top 40 hit 'Almost Grown' and subsequently made a top 100 showing under its own title after being featured in US DJ Alan Freed's rock 'n' roll movie *Go Johnny Go*.

While Paul was the lead vocalist on The Beatles live versions of the song, the likes of The Rolling Stones, Jerry Lee Lewis (with Kid Rock) and REO Speedwagon have all produced versions of the boy/girl song which Berry aimed directly and deliberately at America's youth. "I heard a story for the teen market which had gone so well for me", he explained.

Sweet Little Sixteen

'Sweet Little Sixteen' was issued by Berry in 1958 with

another Beatles favourite – 'Reelin' And Rockin'' – as the B-side. It was to remain Berry's biggest US hit – it reached number two in the charts – until 'My Ding A Ling' topped the charts 14 years later and was a song which also featured in the group's pre-Beatle shows in the late 1950s.

While Eddie Cochran, Joe Brown and The Animals are among the acts who have recorded the song, it was an ex-Beatle who put one of the groups' most popular songs on record. John included it on his successful 1975 album *Rock 'N' Roll* – before it was featured on *Live At The BBC* – while Ringo was on a version with Jerry Lee Lewis in 2006 for the American's *Last Man Standing* collection of duets.

Too Much Monkey Business

'Too Much Monkey Business' became Berry's fifth single when it was issued by Chess in August 1956 with 'Brown Eyed Handsome Man' – a posthumous UK top three hit for Buddy Holly in 1963 – on the B-side.

Once again John took the lead vocal on a song which The Beatles regularly included in their set list from 1960 until 1962. They also began to include other classic Berry songs such as 'Little Queenie', 'Reelin' And Rockin'', 'Rock And Roll Music' and 'Roll Over Beethoven' for the first time. A US R&B top five hit, 'Too Much Monkey Business' appealed to rival British beat groups as The Hollies, The Kinks and The Yardbirds also covered the song alongside Elvis Presley before a 1963 Pop Go The Beatles rendition came out on *Live At The BBC*.

Glad All Over

'Glad All Over' was a song written by Aaron Schroeder, Sid Tepper and Roy Bennett and it was probably Carl Perkins' 1957 Sun recording which prompted The Beatles to include it in their shows from 1960.

According to Paul, Perkins was, "our big idol" while John acknowledged that the American singer and songwriter was "really country, just with more backbeat." But it was George who took the lead on this song for the three years it was part of Beatles concerts. In fact George was such a fan of Perkins that when The Beatles decided in 1960 to (briefly) change their names for showbiz effect George became Carl Harrison.

One of his latest recordings for Sun Records, 'Glad All Over' featured Perkins brothers Jay and Clayton and prompted cover versions by the Jeff Beck Group and The Searchers while George got to perform it with Perkins in a 1985 American TV special ahead of the release of a 1963 live version on *Live At The BBC*.

Lend Me Your Comb

'Lend Me Your Comb' was on the B-side of Perkins' 'Glad All Over' single but made its way into The Beatles live shows in 1960. John and Paul shared the vocals in the style of Carl and Jay Perkins on the song written by Kay Twomey, Fred Wise and Ben Wiesman.

Two of Perkins own compositions also began to creep into The Beatles' set

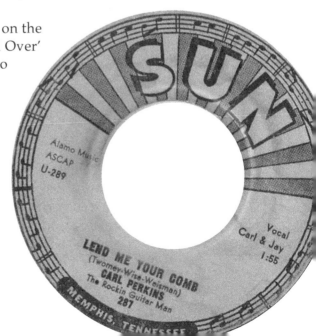

list in 1960 – 'Everybody Trying To Be My Baby' and 'Matchbox' – and both would end up being recorded by the group in 1964, a year after they made the version of 'Lend Me Your Comb' which made it on to *Anthology 1* and two years after The Beatles dropped the song from their live shows.

Sure To Fall

'Sure To Fall (In Love With You)' was co-written by Perkins with Bill Cantrell and Quinton Claunch and appeared on the album *Carl Perkins Dance Album – Teenbeat* which John heard and made a point of playing all the way through as a teenager. Had the track been released, as was planned, as the follow-up to the 1956 hit 'Blue Suede Shoes', which was already in The Beatles' live shows, it could have made it into their set a few years earlier than 1960 when Paul took the lead vocal part.

Dropped in 1963, it was one of the songs The Beatles featured in their unsuccessful audition for Decca Records on January 1 1962 and Ringo included it – with Paul McCartney guesting – on his 1981 album *Stop And The Smell The Roses* ahead of the *Live At The BBC* release of a 1963 *Pop Go The Beatles* version.

Your True Love

'Your True Love' became Perkins's last hit on the Sun label when it peaked at number 67 in April 1957 with 'Matchbox' as the B-side. George began taking the lead vocals in the days before The Beatles hit the road and continued to sing it through to the end of 1962.

Jerry Lee Lewis played piano on the original recording but left the cover versions to Gene Simons, Rick Nelson and Chris Isaak while George performed the song at Perkins funeral in 1998.

I Got A Woman

'I Got A Woman' was written by Ray Charles and his (originally uncredited) band member Renald Richard and had been released by Charles in 1954 without making any impression on the charts in either the US or the UK. But it was probably the version Elvis Presley included on his first album which inspired The Beatles to feature as part of their live shows in 1960.

John, who was the biggest Elvis fan – he once declared, "I'm an Elvis fan because it was Elvis who got me out of Liverpool. Once I'd heard it (rock 'n' roll) and got into it, that was life; there was no other thing" – took the lead on the group's stage version.

While Presley was an obvious major influence on The Beatles, Ray Charles also made an impression with George once confirming that the band had liked the blind pianist/singer/songwriter "since the fifties." Charles re-recorded his song under the title 'I Gotta Woman' in 1965 and made it into the US Hot 100 while Bobby Darin, Adam Faith, Roy Orbison, Johnny Cash and Buddy Holly were among the list of cover makers and The Beatles added it to *Live At The BBC*.

THEATRE THREE
PRODUCTIONS

PRESENT
THE FIRST NEW YORK APPEARANCE OF THE

BEATLES
CARNEGIE HALL
WED. FEB. 12

2 SHOWS 7PM & 8·30PM

PRICES $4·00 $4·50 $5·00   TICKETS GO
ON SALE AT CARNGIE HALL FROM JAN 27

I Forgot To Remember To Forget

'I Forgot To Remember To Forget' came from the pens of Stan Kesler and Charlie Feathers and appeared as Presley's fifth Sun single when it was coupled with 'Mystery Train' in October 1955.

It was a number one country & western hit in America and obviously made an impression on The Beatles as – with George on lead vocals – they included it in their shows from 1960 until 1962 alongside other Presley hits such 'All Shook Up', 'Blue Moon Of Kentucky', 'Hound Dog', I't's Now Or Never', 'Jailhouse Rock' and 'Love Me Tender'.

While co-composer Feathers made a version, artists such as Johnny Cash, Jerry Lee Lewis, Johnny Hallyday and Wanda Jackson also covered the song which made it on to The Beatles' *Live At The BBC* with a live version from the 1964 BBC radio show *From Us To You.*

I'm Gonna Sit Right Down And Cry Over You

'I'm Gonna Sit Right Down And Cry Over You' has been described as a "minor pop standard" and the Joe Thomas and Howard Biggs song from 1956 certainly made an impression on The Beatles thanks to Presley's debut chart topping album.

76 From Me To You

Issued in March 1956 the album *Elvis Presley* made it to number one in America at the same time as 'Heartbreak Hotel' was topping the singles chart in the US and reaching number two in the UK. Their impact on The Beatles was summed up by Paul when he said, "Then when we heard the song ('Heartbreak Hotel'), there was the proof. That was followed by the first album which I still love the best of all his records."

Even though John took the lead for three years from 1960 on the group's stage version, it was Paul who re-emphasised what Presley's first long playing record – a million-seller for his new label RCA even before it was even released – meant to the four musician from Liverpool. "It was so fantastic we played it endlessly and tried to learn it all. Everything we did was based on that album."

The Beatles version of the track from 'that' album – recorded in 1963 for *Pop Go The Beatles* – was one of the 69 tracks on *Live At The BBC* double album.

That's Alright (Mama)

'That's Alright (Mama)' was written and recorded in 1946 by Blues singer Arthur 'Big Boy' Crudup and was, memorably, Elvis Presley's first commercial release, being issued by Sun Records in August 1954.

With 'Blue Moon Of Kentucky' as the B-side, the record sold 20,000 and was number one in the local charts in Memphis, Tennessee and both songs were performed by The Silver Beetles and Johnny & The Moondogs in the three years before The Beatles were officially established. Their previously unreleased version of this song made it on to *Live At The BBC*.

Paul, who was the front man on the song throughout the six years it featured in the group's live shows until 1962, admitted in an interview years later just how much influence Presley had on him – "I certainly wanted to be like Elvis."

Searchin'

'Searchin'' was written by the esteemed song writing team of Jerry Lieber and Mike Stoller for R&B and rock 'n' roll group The Coasters in 1957 when it reached number 4 on the US Hot 100.

It earned Carl Gardner, Billy Guy, Bobby Nunn, Young Jessie plus guitarist Adolph Jacobs their first million seller and their first UK hit when it peaked at number 30 and undoubtedly brought the group from Los Angeles to the attention of The Beatles who featured the song in the act from their earliest days.

When he was describing the varied pop scene of the mid 1950s George said, "The pop scene then was mixed. There were the big stars – the Fats Dominos, The Coasters and Elvis – and then artists you heard records by but never really saw much of."

Paul, who sang the lead vocal on stage through to 1962, chose the song as one of his *Desert Island Discs* when he was guest on the BBC radio programme in 1982 and also explained the importance of the song to the band by recalling how they had 'borrowed' the record from a man in Liverpool and never gave it back. "We couldn't return it. We just had to have it, it was like gold dust. 'Searchin''

became a big number with the Beatles."

It also became part of the repertoire of artists such as The Grateful Dead, The Hollies, Neil Sedaka and The Spencer Davis Group and The Beatles' version from their Decca audition on January 1 1962 was part of The Beatles *Anthology 1*.

Three Cool Cats

'Three Cool Cats' was also written by Leiber and Stoller and it featured as the B-side of The Coasters 1959 US and UK top ten hit 'Charlie Brown' which featured new members Cornelius Gunter, Will Jones and sax player King Curtis following the departure of Nunn and Jessie.

While George took the lead on a song The Beatles performed for three years and also included in their Decca audition, it was John who once reflected on the song and the band's appearances on the highly rated BBC radio show *Saturday Club*. "We did a lot of tracks for *Saturday Club*, a lot of stuff we'd been doing in The Cavern or Hamburg. 'Three Cool Cats' I think we did" although oddly the song was not included on the *Live At The BBC* release but their Decca audition version made it on *Anthology 1*.

Young Blood

'Young Blood' also came from the team of Leiber and Stoller with the added talent of writer Doc Pomus – who also wrote with Mort Shulman – and would have caught the ears of the young Beatles when it came out as the B-side of The Coasters' hit 'Searchin'' but earned its own place in the US top ten in 1957 and went on to be covered by the likes of Leon Russell, Bad Company and Jerry Lee Lewis..

Another song which featured in the earliest of pre-Beatle sets and in their Decca audition – this version is on *Anthology 1* – it emphasised the importance to the group of The Coasters and their music as Paul confirmed when he said, quite simply, "We were well into The Coasters."

C'mon Everybody

'C'mon Everybody' was composed by Oklahoma born Eddie Cochran and his song writing partner (and one-time manager) Jerry Capeheart who also featured in a trio alongside Eddie and Hank Cochran, who was no relation to the singer.

Issued on Liberty records in October 1958, 'C'mon Everybody' made it to the US top 40 but more importantly peaked at number six in the UK in April 1959 and immediately became part of The Beatles live shows until the end of 1962. John was moved to say "I saw Eddie Cochran. Eddie Cochran was the only one I saw as a fan, just sitting in the audience."

While Cochran re-recorded the song under the title 'Let's Get Together' – it charted in the UK in 1968 with a version of 'Summertime Blues' – his original was covered by the likes of Led Zeppelin, Cliff Richard, Humble Pie and Sid Vicious.

Hallelujah

'Hallelujah I Love Her So' was written, recorded and released by Ray Charles in 1956 on the Atlantic label and became a top five R&B hit in America but as The Beatles didn't include the song in their shows until 1960 it's likely that it was Eddie Cochran's version – released as a UK top 30 hit in the same year – that made the biggest impression on them and was part of their live show until 1962.

Certainly George was moved by the man and his music. "I saw quite a few shows, the best being the Eddie Cochran one. He was a very good guitar player and that's what I remember most. I was impressed by not only his own songs but by his cover versions like Ray Charles' 'Hallelujah I Love Her So'." An early recorded version from rehearsals in Paul's home – with John, George and Stu Sutcliffe – is on *Anthology 1*

Twenty Flight Rock

'Twenty Flight Rock' was a Cochran co-composition with Ned Fairchild which failed to make any impression in the charts in either the US or the UK when it was released in 1957 but an American movie brought it to the attention of The Beatles as far back as the late 1950s – and they featured on stage through to 1962.

Paul saw *The Girl Can't Help It*, starring buxom actress Jayne Mansfield, and rates it as "still the greatest music film" while Cochran's performance of 'Twenty Flight Rock' made him want to go out and buy the record. "'Twenty Flight Rock' was a hard record to get; I remember ordering it and having to wait weeks for it to come in." But having got it, he set about learning the song which later the same year would change his life for ever.

In July 1957 he was at the Woolton Village Fete watching the Quarry Men perform when he met John Lennon backstage and began playing piano before switching instruments. "Then I played the guitar – upside down. I did 'Twenty Flight Rock' and knew all the words. The Quarry Men were so knocked out that I actually knew and could sing 'Twenty Flight Rock'. That's what got me into The Beatles."

The man who made such an impression on George – "I remember Eddie Cochran well: he had his black leather waistcoat, black leather trousers and a raspberry coloured shirt" – and provided Paul with his passport to The Beatles died following a car crash in Britain on April 17, the day after Cochran had finished a ten-week tour of the UK together with Gene Vincent.

Lucille

'Lucille' became Little Richard's sixth US top 30 hit and first British top ten hit when it was released in June 1957. Credited to Richard – under his real Richard Penniman – and Al Collins, it was rumoured that the song was written solely by Collins who sold his interest to Little Richard while serving time in prison.

Coupled with 'Send Me Some Lovin'', 'Lucille' was also featured in the film *The Girl Can't Help It* along with Little Richard who also appeared in the earlier movie *Don't Knock The Rock* and had a major impact on The Beatles who were being heavily influenced by

American rhythm and blues. "I think we, The Beatles, were initially Elvis-y, Gene Vincent-y, Little Richard-y, Chuck Berry, Fats Domino", said Paul.

Covered by AC/DC, Queen, Van Halen and Waylon Jennings, who had a surprise number one US country hit in 1983, Paul included the song on an album of rock 'n' roll favourites he recorded exclusively for release in Russia in 1988 before a Beatles version from *Saturday Club* in 1963 made it on to *Live At The BBC*.

Ooh My Soul

'Ooh My Soul' – written and recorded by Little Richard – was released in June 1958, two years ahead of his debut UK tour and an appearance at the Tower Ballroom New Brighton with The Beatles and other Mersey beat acts such as Billy J Kramer & The Dakotas and the Merseybeats.

While the record peaked outside the US top 20 and failed to make the UK top 30, it made an impact on The Beatles who featured Paul as lead vocalist on their live performances between 1960 and 1962.

In late 1962, Richard shared the bill with The Beatles during a 14-day stint at Hamburg's Star Club and made a lasting impression on the Beatles new drummer. "I watched Little Richard twice a night for six days; it was so great.

He did show off a bit in front of us," said Ringo. A version recorded at the Manchester Playhouse Theatre in1963 for *Pop Go The Beatles* is on *Live At The BBC*.

Be-Bop-A-Lula

'Be-Bop-A-Lula' was originally issued as the B-side of Gene Vincent's debut single 'Woman Love', released by Capitol in June 1956, but radio reaction forced the label to switch the record. Written by Vincent and his manager Bill Davis (although there are stories that he actually bought the rights to the song from the original co-writer Donald Graven and then credited himself as a co-writer) it was recorded by Vincent and his group The Blue Caps and reached number seven in the US Hot 100, selling a reported two million copies in an under a year.

A feature of The Beatles' live shows for three years, another song from the film *The Girl Can't Help It*, also holds a special memory for Paul. He recalls that "'Be-Bop-A-Lula' … was the first record I ever bought" while John remembered seeing Vincent perform on stage in Hamburg … and being disappointed with what he saw and heard. "When Gene Vincent did 'Be-Bop-A-Lula' in Hamburg He didn't do it the same. It was a thrill to meet Gene Vincent and see him but it was not 'Be-Bop-A-Lula'. I'm a record fan."

Vincent, in turn, had his own memories of meeting and playing with the four musicians from Liverpool in Hamburg. "It's OK here. I had a nice band backing me. They're called The Beatles." In addition to cover versions by David Cassidy, Queen and the Everly Bothers, two Beatles produced their own solo recordings in the years after the group split. John opened his *Rock 'N' Roll* album with the song and Paul followed suit by including as the first track on his 1991 *Unplugged* (the Official Bootleg) album.

Dance In The Street

'Dance In The Street' was one of the four tracks by Vincent which made up a 1958 EP featuring songs from a movie called *Hot Rod Gang* which was later re-titled *Fury Unleashed* for release in the UK. It was recorded during the sessions for Vincent's fourth album *A Gene Vincent Record Date* alongside 'Baby Blue', 'Lovely Loretta' and 'Dance To The Bop' when Eddie Cochran appeared as an uncredited backing vocalist.

As Vincent and his Blue Caps appeared and performed the song in the film and The Beatles were ardent fans of music films its possible that they picked up the song from the movie and added it to their repertoire in 1960 (until 1962) with the lead vocal falling to John who once outlined another influence Vincent had on the young Beatles. "...we bought leather pants and looked like four Gene Vincents – only a bit younger."

In reply Vincent assessed the fab four's music in the early sixties by saying "...the stuff the Beatles sing is rock 'n' roll but a bit noisier."

Dark Town Strutters' Ball

"Dark Town Strutters' Ball' was one of the more bizarre songs covered by The Beatles during their Cavern and Hamburg days. Written by Shelton Brooks in 1917, it was considered a jazz standard and recorded by minstrel/comedy singer Arthur Collins

in 1918 followed by The Jimmy Dorsey Orchestra, Pee Wee Hunt and Fats Waller before Joe Brown recorded as his third single for Decca.

English-born singer and multi instrumentalist Brown – who began his career as a backing musician on the pioneering TV show *Boy Meets Girl* (where he played with Eddie Cochran and Gene Vincent) – and his group The Bruvvers had a number 34 hit in the UK with the song in 1960 and that is probably how it came to the attention of The Beatles who were familiar with Brown's rock 'n' roll recordings.

"Joe Brown had done a rock 'n' roll version of the 'Sheik Of Araby'" said George referring to the idea of turning an old song into a rock song. "That was the thing to do if you didn't have a tune; just rock up an oldie. I did the Joe Brown records," added the man who sang lead on 'Dark Town Strutters' Ball'.

Even though The Beatles performed the song on stage between 1960 and 1962 they never recorded it although a version of the song appeared on a 1964 album entitled *The Beatles With Tony Sheridan & Their Guests* when it was recorded by US session group The Titans who added six tracks to five by Sheridan and The Beatles – or Beat Boys as they were called – on the US top 70 chart hit.

Nothin' Shakin' (But The Leaves On The Trees)

'Nothin' Shakin' (But The Leaves On The Trees)' was originally created in 1958 by singer/actor Eddie Fontaine although he later shared the

composer's credit with Cirino Colacrai, Diane Lampert and John Gluck.

Fontaine released the single on the Sunbeam label in 1958 and it made its way into the US top 70, a year after his appearance in Paul's favourite music movie *The Girl Can't Help It*. The Beatles gave 'Nothin' Shakin'' to George to sing on stage between 1960 and 1962 and later featured it on the album *Live At The BBC*

In 1955 Fontaine had been such a draw that pioneering US disc jockey Alan Freed included him on the bill of his first ever Rock 'n' Roll Jubilee concert at Brooklyn's famous Paramount Theatre and 'Nothin' Shakin'' was covered by Dr Feelgood, Billy Fury and Billy Craddock who turned it into a US top ten country hit.

(I Do The) Shimmy Shimmy

'(I Do The) Shimmy Shimmy' was a Top 40 hit in America in 1960 for soul/R&B singer Bobby Freeman and it came between his only two top five hits 'Do You Wanna Dance' – which was covered as 'Do You Want To Dance' by John Lennon (on his *Rock'N'Roll* album), Del Shannon and Cliff Richard – and 'C'mon And Swim'.

With John and Paul sharing vocals on the Bill Marsden and Andy Shubert song, 'Shimmy Shimmy' was included in The Beatles shows for three years from 1960 and perhaps recognised San Franciso-born Freeman's position as a regular on America's early rock 'n 'roll package tours and as a purveyor of 'latin rock' songs alongside Richie Valens, Marty Robins and The Drifters.

Crying, Waiting, Hoping

'Crying, Waiting, Hoping' was one of the last four songs recorded by Buddy Holly, less than a month before his death in a plane crash in February 1959. On January 22, with just his guitar, he sang four numbers into a tape recorder in his apartment in New York's Greenwich Village before leaving for a tour with Richie Valens and The Big Bopper.

It was released in August 1959 as the B-side to 'Peggy Sue Got Married' and reached number 13 in the US but by then Holly, who toured the UK and appeared on British TV shows in 1958, had become a major influence on The Beatles both as a performer and a songwriter. "Buddy Holly was completely different, he was out of Nashville so that introduced us to the country music scene", said Paul who added, "I still like Buddy's vocal style. And his writing."

While The Beatles only recorded one of Holly's songs ('Words Of Love') they featured his music – 'It's So Easy', 'Maybe Baby', 'Peggy Sue', 'That'll Be The Day' and 'Think It Over' – in their shows from their earliest pre-Beatles days. A live recording of 'Crying Waiting Hoping' from the 1963 show *Pop Go The Beatles* featured on the *Live At The BBC* release.

Clarabella

'Clarabella' was written by Frank Pingatore and recorded by The Jodimars in 1956 on the Capitol label. The group were formed when Joey Ambrose, Dick Bocelli and Marshall Lyle left Bill Haley's Rockets over a wages dispute and teamed

up with Chuck Hess, Max Daffner and Jim Buffington to form a new group.

The Rockets' (plus Haley) version of 'Rock Around The Clock' was part of the movie *The Blackboard Jungle* which Paul saw together with an under-age George and he recalled the impact it had on him. "The first time I heard that shivers went down my spine so we had to go and see the film."

Perhaps impressed by their work with Haley, Paul sang the lead vocal on 'Clarabella' for three years until 1962 and it also features on *Live At The BBC*. He also recalls that it was one of the more obscure songs they performed live for George Martin at EMI in 1962. "I think we probably played them all to George. 'Clarabella' was one."

Well Baby Please Don't Go

'Well Baby Please Don't Go' was issued in 1958 as the B-side of the US number 8 hit and UK top ten entry 'Western Movies' by The Olympics. It was written by Walter Ward, the leader of the Los Angeles-based doo-wop band which featured Eddie Lewis, Charles Fizer, Walter Hammond and Melvin King and also hit the charts in 1961 with 'I Wish I Could Shimmy Like My Sister Kate'.

John once recalled the decision to switch from covers such as obscure Olympics' tracks to performing their own compositions. "It was a quite traumatic thing because we were doing great numbers of other people's songs. I used to do an old Olympics number called 'Well at the Cavern', a twelve bar thing."

A regular in Beatles live shows in 1960, 1961 and 1962 – but not included on *Live At The BBC* nor any of the Beatles Anthology collections – 'Well Baby Please Don't Go' was featured on two posthumous John Lennon releases – the 1998 collections *John Lennon Anthology* and *Wonsaponatime*.

Hippy Hippy Shake

'Hippy Hippy Shake' is best remembered as a number two UK hit for Liverpool band The Swinging Blue Jeans in 1963 but it was originally recorded in 1959 by American rock 'n' roller Chan (Robert) Romero and it was this version which inspired The Beatles to include it – with Paul taking the lead – in live shows from 1961 until 1963.

As The Beatles began to focus on their own compositions songs such as 'Hippy Hippy Shake', 'If You Gotta Make A Fool Of Somebody', 'You Were Meant For Me' and 'Some Other Guy' passed from their stage act to become hits for other acts. "We couldn't record it all when we did get a deal", recalled Paul, "so other groups took songs from our acts and made hits out of them – like The Swinging Blue Jeans with 'Hippy Hippy Shake' which was one of my big numbers."

But The Beatles it seems were not people to hold a grudge as when John, Paul, George and Ringo appeared as judges on the BBC TV show *Juke Box Jury* in December 1963 they voted the Swinging Blue Jeans' version a resounding hit.

Red Sails In The Sunset

'Red Sails In The Sunset' was composed by Hugh Williams (born George Grosz) and James Kennedy – an Austrian/English

writing team – whose 1935 song was recorded by Al Bowlly and Ray Noble before World War II.

While Nat King Cole (1951) and Fat Domino (1963) recorded hit versions, it was Big Joe Turner's 1957 interpretation which possibly influenced The Beatles who were fans of his rock classic 'Shake Rattle And Roll' which he first recorded in 1954, ahead of Bill Haley, Carl Perkins and Elvis Presley. They would also have been familiar with Emile Ford and The Checkmates' version made in 1960 as he headlined a show with The Beatles in New Brighton in April 1962.

Although Turner, who appeared in the film *Shake Rattle And Roll*, never had a hit with 'Red Sails In The Sunset' and The Beatles never included it in any of their later collections, Paul sang lead vocals on the song throughout the period from 1960 to 1962.

Songs the Beatles gave away

As song writers John Lennon and Paul McCartney were, to say the least, prolific so it will come as no surprise to learn that they wrote songs – both together and individually – which they considered unsuitable for The Beatles and were prepared to offer to other artists

Confirming what we all knew already Paul McCartney once said, "John and I were a song writing team and what

song writing teams did in those days was write for everyone. John and I would get together 'Oh we gotta write one for Billy J, OK' … and we just knocked them out." And some years earlier his partner John Lennon had explained, "We used to write mainly on tour. We got bored so we wrote."

Many of the songs The Beatles never used and eventually gave away ended up, perhaps not surprisingly, being recorded and released by acts managed by their own guiding light, Brian Epstein. The manager of The Beatles, it seems, was never slow in encouraging the two leading song writers in his stable to pass on an unwanted song to one of the other artists he controlled – and in the process delivering them a much-wanted chart hit.

In addition to the pop hits, there were other compositions which – even though they were written during the time The Beatles still existed and credited in the main to their own Northern Songs publishing operation – were clearly never intended for the 'fab four.' Many of them were often written, as were so many of the Lennon/McCartney 'joint' compositions, by a solo John or Paul. Similarly George Harrison also chose to pass on a couple of his songs to acts who he thought would prosper from his efforts.

Here is a breakdown of 25 songs which were written between 1957 and 1969– the year in which The Beatles recorded together for the last time – and 'given away'. They range from the chart successes of a handful of fellow Liverpudlian acts (plus a few other stars of the swinging sixties) to odd throwaway songs and orchestral theme tunes, plus compositions which were intended to help establish artists signed to the group's own Apple label in the run up to the day when the Beatles were finally no more.

We start with the two acts who each recorded four Lennon and McCartney songs and while one was a group who were rivals (and friends) from Liverpool, the other was a couple of ex-public schoolboys who had a unique relationship with one of the song writing team. And from there – after an ex-cloakroom girl and a jolly foursome – we head through a list of groups and singers who have one unreleased 'Beatles song' to their credit.

Billy J Kramer & The Dakotas

I'll Be On My Way

Bad To Me

I'll Keep You Satisfied

From A Window

Billy J Kramer & The Dakotas were formed in Liverpool after Kramer was spotted by local manager Brian Epstein playing at the famous Cavern club with local band The Coasters. When Epstein – who bought Kramer's contract from a rival local promoter for £50 – failed to team him with The Coasters on a permanent basis (the group were reluctant to give up their day jobs) he turned to Manchester band The Dakotas – made up of Mike Maxfield (lead guitar), Robin MacDonald (rhythm guitar), Ray Jones (bass) & Tony Mansfield (drums) – to create a new group for his management stable.

In 1963 the group were signed to EMI's

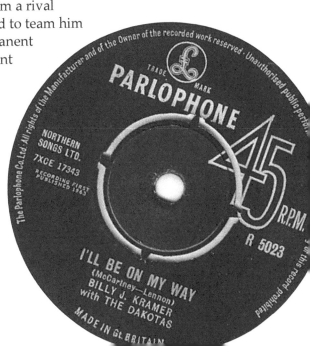

Parlophone label where producer George Martin added them to his ever increasing list of acts, although he had doubts about the singer. "Billy's voice wasn't the strongest or best in the world so I decided to always double track him and I used a wound up piano to cover some of the bad notes," he explained.

With a new letter added to his name – the story goes that it was John Lennon who suggested that the letter J was inserted and also said that Kramer could explain to people that it stood for Julian, the name of Lennon's son – Billy J Kramer recorded the Lennon/McCartney song 'Do You Want To Know A Secret?' which had appeared on their debut *Please Please Me* album as his debut single. It reached number two in the UK in June 1964 where it stalled behind The Beatles 'From Me To You'.

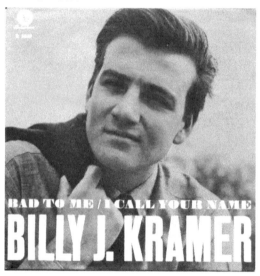

On the B-side of the record was an unused song written by McCartney called 'I'll Be On My Way' – which was never recorded by the group but was performed by The Beatles on the BBC Radio Show *Side By Side* in April 1963.

Kramer's next choice of song was 'Bad To Me' which was written specially for him by Lennon while he was on holiday in Spain.

Although it was never recorded by The Beatles, Lennon did make a demo disc of the song which Kramer eventually took to the top of the British chart for three weeks in August 1963 and went on to become a US top ten hit in July 1964.

After being voted Best British Newcomer in the 1963 Melody Maker poll, Kramer – whose real name was William Ashton – turned to a McCartney song 'I'll Keep You Satisfied' for his third single which peaked at number four in the UK in October 1963 and reached number 30 in American.

In August 1964 another Lennon/McCartney song 'From A Window' became the group's fifth single. It was released after Jones left the band to be replaced by ex-Johnny Kidd & Pirates guitarist Mick Green and hit the UK top ten and the US top thirty.

After the group released their last single in 1966, Kramer pursued a solo career and asked McCartney for a song to help him get back into the limelight but when he was offered a new composition called 'Yesterday', he turned it down. In recent years Kramer recorded a children's album (2005) plus a contemporary album (2012) and he also wrote a successful graphic novel in 2013.

Peter & Gordon

A World Without Love

Nobody I Know

I Don't Want To See You

Woman

Peter & Gordon consisted of Peter Asher, the former child actor and brother of Paul McCartney's actress girl-friend Jane Asher,

and Gordon Waller. They were both doctors sons and attended Westminster School together where they started out as the folk duo Gordon & Peter.

After being spotted by EMI producer Norman Newell, they were

invited to record a song called 'If I Were You' as their debut single for EMI, but instead Asher decided to ask his sister's boyfriend if he had a song they could record. McCartney opted to give them a new song he was still working on called 'A World Without Love' – which they recorded in Abbey Road with Newell as producer.

Reviewed in New Musical Express, the record was described as "a disc which could easily register in the chart, if only because of its Beatles association" although the reviewer did suggest that it was "not one of John and Paul's greatest song, but it's still quite effective." It went to number one in the UK in April 1964 and topped the US chart two months later, racking up global sales of over one million. The duo's next single was another McCartney song entitled 'Nobody I Know' which was also a million-seller, peaking at number ten in the UK and reaching number 12 in America.

Their third single was McCartney's 'I Don't Want To See You' – and like all the others it was credited to Lennon/McCartney – which failed to chart in UK but reached the US top twenty in October 1964.

After a further three hits with non-Lennon/McCartney songs, Peter & Gordon returned to McCartney and recorded his song 'Woman', which was credited to Bernard Webb as part of an experiment to see how his songs would work if they weren't credited to Lennon/McCartney. It reached the UK top thirty and in America, where the song was credited to a composer called A.Smith, it peaked at number 14 in March 1966.

The duo of Peter & Gordon finally broke up in 1967, but reunited briefly a year later before going their separate ways with Asher becoming A&R manager of The Beatles' Apple Records in 1968 and signing and producing James Taylor. He left in 1969 to become a hugely successful US-based manager and award winning producer, while Waller ran a gift store in Cornwall before they briefly reunited again in 2008 and 2009, the year when Waller died aged 64.

Cilla Black

Love Of The Loved

It's For You

Step Inside Love

Liverpool girl Priscilla White was a cloakroom attendant and occasional singer at the famous Cavern club – where she was billed as "Swinging Cilla" – when she was

spotted by producer George Martin while he was checking out a local group called Gerry & Pacemakers. After an early edition of the local Mersey Beat magazine had mistakenly printed her name as Cilla Black instead of Cilla White, the singer opted for a new identity.

She was signed to Parlophone by Martin in summer 1963 and agreed a management deal with Brian Epstein in September of the same year after auditioning with The Beatles in a local club. Her first release was a very early McCartney song entitled 'Love Of The Loved' which had been part of The Beatles live set from the late

1950s through to 1962. On the back of her TV debut on *Ready Steady Go* in September 1963, the record reached the UK top 40

In her autobiography *What's It All About* (Ebury Press 2003), Black recalled that in early press interviews she had claimed that the song had been specially written for her by John and Paul. "But of course it was cobblers," she wrote. "I'd heard the lads doing the number themselves during lunchtime sessions at the Cavern so I knew it wasn't a new song. But even if the song was off the peg it suited my voice and the recording had come out good."

While producer George Martin recalled Black as a "screeching yelling rock 'n' roll singer", he acknowledged who it was who changed her style. "It was Brian (Epstein) who decided to she could be a ballad singer."

After two hits with non-Lennon & McCartney songs, Black

recorded McCartney's 'It's For You' in July 1964 when both Lennon and McCartney were in the studio and the composer played piano on the recording. McCartney later recalled, "'It's For You' was something else, that was something I'd written. You sometimes would pull one out of the drawer and say 'maybe this would be good for you'."

In her book Black explained, "Paul introduced me to the song by sending a demo disc that'd he made of it round to the Palladium (she was in an eight month season with The Fourmost and Frankie Vaughan). Although Paul had sung it as a waltz, George Martin took a big hand in my recording of it and asked Johnny Spence (Tom Jones' musical director) to arrange it. It was a fabulous arrangement."

And, according to Black, on the day of the recording two people turned up unannounced in the studio. "John and Paul, who had only arrived back that morning from Australia, came round to Abbey Road. It was great to see them. They were in awe of Johnny Spence as well as George Martin so they didn't dare to interfere with the recording." The record peaked at number seven in the UK but only just reached the top 80 in America.

In January 1968, Black's new BBC TV series was launched with a new McCartney song called 'Step Inside Love' which he had specially written as the theme for the show, although it would be a further two months before it was released as a single. Even though McCartney had done a demo of the song, Black explained the reason for the delay, "This was because Paul's songs, although simple in essence, were often difficult to arrange and get the sound

that was wanted, and he had left writing it until the last moment." At the recording in a studio in London's Bond Street, Paul played guitar and the record went to number eight in the UK and returned her to the UK top ten after an absence of nearly two years.

While Black continued recording – her last hit was in 1993 – she also achieved new success as a host on TV shows such as *Blind Date* and *Surprise Surprise* which led to her becoming Britain's highest paid female TV star.

The Fourmost

Hello Little Girl

I'm In Love

The Fourmost were Brian O'Harra (guitar/vocals), Mike Millward (guitar/vocals), Billy Hatton (bass) & Dave Lovelady (drums) and they first got together in Liverpool as The Blue Jays before becoming The Four Jays and then, in 1962, The Four Mosts. When Brian Epstein took over their management in 1963 he changed their name again – this time

to The Fourmost – and got them a recording deal with Parlophone.

Their first record was an unused Lennon/McCartney song 'Hello Little Girl' which Lennon had written in late 1957. "This was one of the first songs I ever finished. I was then about 18 and we gave it to the Fourmost," he explained. In fact it was a song which The Beatles had included in their stage act from 1957 through to 1962 but it was when The Fourmost appeared with The Beatles at the Queen's Theatre in Blackpool on August 1963 that Lennon told them that they could have 'Hello Little Girl', which had also been part of the group's Decca audition in January 1962.

Group member Billy Hatton told 'Mersey Beat' magazine that after they had met up at John's house and been shown the words to the song, John and George gave them a rough idea of how it sounded by taping the tune. But with The Fourmost set to go into the studio to record the song, Hatton recalled, "We had two days in which to make an arrangement good enough to put on disc. As a matter of fact when we were recording, we were just learning the song as we went along and were tremendously encouraged by A&R man George Martin."

The record hit number nine in the UK in October 1963, just before The Fourmost appeared in *The Beatles Christmas Show* and released their second single. 'I'm In Love' which was a song either written especially for them by both Lennon & McCartney or (depending on which source you believe) an early pre-Beatles Lennon solo effort which Epstein obtained for The Fourmost.

Either way it peaked at number 17 in the UK in December 1963 and brought to an end the group's association with Lennon and McCartney the song writers.

After founding member Millward died aged 23 in 1966, the quartet ended their recording career in 1969 but not before McCartney had helped them out again – this time as the producer of a song he had discovered called 'Rosetta'. But even with McCartney playing piano, the disc failed to chart and The Fourmost were relegated to the cabaret circuit until they finally split up in 1978.

The Applejacks

Like Dreamers Do

Birmingham group The Applejacks consisted of Al Jackson (vocals), Martin Baggot (guitar), Phil Cash (rhythm guitar), Don Gould (organ), Gary Freeman (drums) and – unusual for the time – female bass player Megan Davies.

They were first of the so-called Brumbeat groups to reach the UK top ten when they hit number seven with their debut single 'Tell Me When' in March 64. Their follow up single was a song called 'Like Dreamers Do' which was written for them by McCartney.

The group had met The Beatles at the rehearsals for a TV show and claimed that they were then offered the song by The Beatles who had featured it in their live shows from 1957. However another possibility is that the song was chosen for The Applejacks by Mike Smith – their A&R manager at Decca – who had been on The Beatles' audition session in January 1962 when they performed the title as an example of their songwriting ability.

The Applejacks' version of 'Like Dreamers Do' peaked at number 20 in the UK June 1964, four months before they notched up their final hit, and the band ceased recording in 1967.

Badfinger

Come And Get It

Badfinger emerged out of the Liverpool group The Iveys and were recommended to McCartney by The Beatles road manager Mal Evans. As a result Pete Ham (guitar), Tom Evans (rhythm guitar), Mike Gibbons (bass) and Rob Griffiths (drums) signed to Apple Records and became Badfinger after McCartney recalled that the original title of the song 'With a Little Help From My Friends' was 'Badfinger Boogie'.

Their debut release on The Beatles' record label was 'Maybe Tomorrow' in November 1968 but they had to wait until January 1970 for their first hit when they recorded McCartney's song 'Come And Get It'. It ended up being used on the soundtrack of Ringo Starr's film *The Magic Christian* although the drummer later admitted, "Badfinger did the title track. How they got there I don't know. It wasn't through me."

In fact the original plan was for The Beatles to record the song and McCartney did a demo in Abbey Road on July 24 1969 ahead of the group's afternoon session when

they recorded the tracks 'Sun King' and 'Mean Mr Mustard' for their album Abbey Road.

Eventually the composer took it to Badfinger and insisted "It's got to be exactly like this demo." However, the group apparently had some ideas of their own on how the song should sound but McCartney told them, "It's perhaps a little bit undignified for you, a little bit lacking in integrity to have to copy someone's work that rigidly, but this is the hit sound."

And he was right as the version he produced for the group in Abbey Road studios on August 2 1969 reached number four in the UK chart. Badfinger were Apple's most successful act – after The Beatles – and appeared at *The Concert For Bangladesh* in1971 and on Lennon's *Imagine* album and Harrison's *All Thing Must Pass*. However, after writing the hugely successful song 'Without You' (a number one for Nilsson in 1972 and Mariah Carey in 1994) Ham committed suicide in 1975 and Evans did the same in 1983.

Chris Barber & his Jazz Band

Catcall

Chris Barber & his Jazz Band recorded McCartney's instrumental track 'Catcall' in June 1967 but, despite the composer and his girlfriend Jane Asher attending the recording session –and even adding piano and some odd background vocals – it failed to chart. It was originally titled 'Catwalk' when McCartney wrote it in late fifties and was featured in live performances by both The Quarrymen and The Beatles.

Band leader and trombonist Barber had appeared in Liverpool during Britain's jazz and skiffle boom in the late 1950s when he featured the up and coming skiffle star Lonnie Donegan – an early inspiration for both McCartney and Harrison – in his line-up.

The track Catcall appeared on Barber's 1969 album *Battersea Fair Dance* and in 2009 when Barber got together with fellow-jazzers Acker Bilk and Kenny Ball for a one-off show at London's O2 Arena.

The Black Dyke Mills Band

Thingumybob

Yorkshire brass band The Black Dyke Mills Band was chosen by McCartney to record his composition 'Thingumybob' which he had written as the theme for a 1968 TV comedy series starring actor Stanley Holloway.

McCartney went to Bradford to arrange, produce and record the single which was issued on the Apple label in September 1968. It failed to chart and was the band's only Apple release although they did appear on Wings album *Back To The Egg* where they played on 'Winter Rose' and 'Love Awake'.

"I've always loved brass bands so I wrote and produced a song for the Black Dyke Mills Band. We went up north to Saltaire near Bradford. I wanted a really different sound so we went out and played it on the streets. It was lovely with very dead, trumpety-sounding cornets," recounted McCartney. At the same

time the brass band recorded a more familiar Beatles song after McCartney had apparently told the band's conductor Geoffrey Brand, "Do an arrangement for 'Yellow Submarine' as well. We'll put that on the back." However, when the single was released in America, things were reversed and 'Thingumybob' was relegated to the B-side.

Formed in Queensbury, West Yorkshire in 1855, when they were named John Foster & Son Black Dyke Mills Band, they have been crowned both UK and European Brass Band champions.

Mary Hopkin

Goodbye

Welsh folk singer Mary Hopkin was brought to McCartney's attention by famous model Twiggy who had seen her appearances on a TV talent show. After seeing the singer for himself on *Opportunity Knocks*,

McCartney was convinced that she was an interesting new talent. "I thought she really had got a lovely Welsh voice, it was very well pitched. And she looked nice with a folky guitar."

After she had won the contest, McCartney set about tracing her in an effort to sign her to Apple and he explained in an interview with Melody Maker that when he rang her and asked if she would be interested in recording for the Beatles new label, she said "Would you like to speak to my mother?"

After she had signed-up, Hopkin came to London where McCartney produced her first single 'Those Were The Days' which became the second release on Apple Records following The Beatles' 'Hey Jude'. It went to number one in the UK (after Hey Jude), reached number two in America (behind Hey Jude) in August 1968 and sold over five million copies worldwide.

Declaring that "Mary Hopkin was the main artist whom I produced at Apple", McCartney then wrote the song 'Goodbye' as her follow-up single. After making a demo of the track, he also produced the record which reached number five in the UK and made the American top 20. After her Apple career disintegrated, Hopkin married (and divorced) record producer Tony Visconti and also appeared on David Bowie's *Low* album in 1977.

Jackie Lomax

Sour Milk Sea

Jackie Lomax was a member of the popular Liverpool group The Undertakers – they appeared in mourning coats and top hats – who reached the UK top 50 in 1964 with 'Just A Little Bit'. Later with his band the Lomax Alliance, he signed a management deal with Brian Epstein and, after

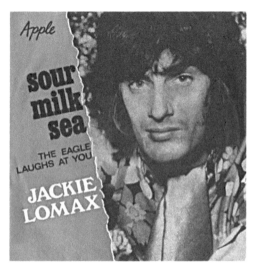

Epstein's death in 1967, he signed to Apple Record as a solo singer.

His debut single – one of the label's first four releases in August 1968 – was the song 'Sour Milk Sea' which had been written by George Harrison during The Beatles visit to India in February 1968 to see the Maharishi Mahesh Yogi. It was never offered up as a potential Beatles track and instead Lomax recorded it with McCartney on piano, Nicky Hopkins on piano, Eric Clapton on guitar, Ringo Starr on drums plus George Harrison on rhythm guitar.

However, despite the superstar line-up, the record was a flop and Lomax eventually left Apple and moved to America where he recorded for both Warner Bros. and Capitol Records and also sang with the group Badger.

George Martin Orchestra

Love In the Open Air

While George Martin spent many years producing records for The Beatles – he even played on a few – his instrumental orchestral versions of their songs appeared on a selection of albums including four tracks on the US number one version of the group's *A Hard Day's Night* album.

In 1967 the tables were turned when McCartney wrote the score for the film *The Family Way* (starring Hayley Mills, Hywel Bennett and John Mills) and invited Martin to work with him. "Film scores were an interesting diversion for me and with George Martin being able to write and orchestrate – and being pretty good at it – I got an offer from the Boulting Brothers for him and me to do some film music for *The Family Way*."

And McCartney knew exactly what he had in mind for the film's score. "I wanted brass band music; because with The Beatles we got into a lot of different kinds of music, but maybe brass was a little too Northern and "Hovis". For the film I got something together that was sort of 'brassy bandy', to echo the Northerness of the story and I had a great time.

The music was recorded by the eleven-piece George Martin Orchestra and the 15 track soundtrack album – which also featured McCartney on piano and bass – was released in Jan 1967 with the single 'Love In the Open Air' being issued in both the UK & US.

While neither the album or the single charted, Paul later recalled, "We got an Ivor Novello Award for the score – for the best film song that year, a piece called 'Love In The Open Air' which Johnny Mercer was nearly going to put lyrics to but I didn't know who he was. I should have done that."

Jotta Herre/ Carlos Mendes

Penina

The story goes that Portugese band Jotta Herre were handed the song

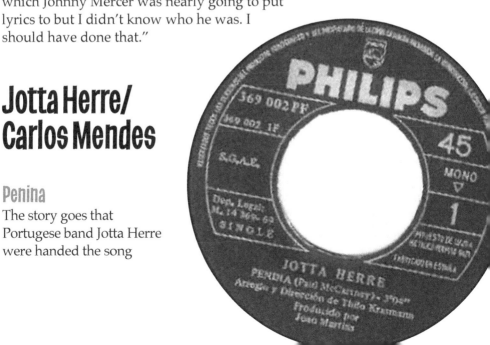

'Penina' by McCartney during one of the singer's holidays in Portugal. The composition was named after the luxury Hotel Penina on the Algarve coast where he was staying and the band were the regular in-house entertainment.

Explaining the story behind the song, McCartney later said, "One night, when I had already had a few drinks, I drank some more in the hotel bar. There was a band playing and I ended up playing the drums. The hotel was called Penina and I improvised a song with that name. Somebody asked me if (s)he could have it and I accepted. I never thought about recording it myself".

During the same holiday in late 1968, it seems that Portugese singer Carlos Mendes (or Mendez) also discovered the song and he asked McCartney if he could record it. Despite being told by the composer that he could "have it", The Beatles' publishing company Northern Songs stepped in when they heard the story and contacted Mendes, who had previously been lead singer with a group called The Sheiks, to tell him the bad news – he couldn't have it after all.

After some lengthy negotiations, Mendes' version was finally released in July 1969 – but only in Portugal – although it seems that the local band Jotta Herre beat him to it and released their version a few months earlier.

PJ Proby

That Means A Lot

Texas-born singer PJ Proby (real name James Marcus Smith) had notched up five UK top 20 hits between May 1964 and September 1965 before he was offered a genuine joint Lennon/McCartney song.

'That Means A Lot' was left over from the *Help* film and album sessions and after The Beatles had recorded it on February 20 1965 (and again on March 20), Lennon was reported as saying, "The song is a

P. J. PROBY

THAT MEANS A LOT
MY PRAYER

ballad which Paul and I wrote for the film but we found we just couldn't sing it. In fact we made a hash of it so we thought we'd better give it to someone who could do it well" while Paul explained, "There were a few songs that we were just not as keen on or we didn't think they were quite finished. This was one of them."

Proby – who appeared on The Beatles TV special *Around The Beatles* in April 1964 – eventually got the song after he asked the two Beatles for one of their spare compositions. He also asked them to try and persuade George Martin to produce it but in the end he had to make do with Martin's Abbey Road sidekick Ron Richards (producer of The Hollies). The record, which was made on April 7 1965, peaked at number 30 in the UK in September of that year.

Famous for his trouser splitting activities – at one time he was banned from all the ABC theatres in Britain – Proby last hit the charts in the UK in 1968 but later appeared in Roy Orbison and Elvis Presley tribute musicals before embarking on a series of sixties nostalgia tours.

Tommy Quickly

Tip Of My Tongue

Liverpool telephone fitter Tommy Quigley was

TIP OF MY TONGUE
(Lennon, McCartney)
NORTHERN SONGS

PICCADILLY

7N.3513

RECORDING FIRST
PUBLISHED 1963
P.45.1137-A

TOMMY QUICKLY
Accompaniment directed by
LES REED

spotted by Brian Epstein when he appeared as Johnny Quickly and the Challengers on a Beatles show at the Queens Hall, Widnes in autumn 1962. A year later he signed with Epstein, became a solo singer named Tommy Quickly and appeared on three Beatles package tours and a Christmas special.

Epstein devoted a lot of time and money in trying to break Quickly including giving him Lennon/McCartney songs to record. The first was Lennon's 'No Reply' (from album *Beatles For Sale*) which the group abandoned after a reported 17 takes had produced nothing worth releasing.

He was then given the McCartney song 'Tip Of My Tongue' which The Beatles had featured in their live shows in 1962 and also recorded on November 26 1962 as a possible track for their debut *Please Please Me* LP and as a potential B-side to the title track single.

It was recorded during afternoon and evening sessions in several takes but producer George Martin was unhappy with the arrangement and suggested that it should be held for another day ... but The Beatles never went back to it and Quickly took it on.

But despite a major campaign led by Epstein and Pye Records

Piccadilly label, Quickly's July 1963 version still failed to chart. He eventually achieved a chart hit in October 1964 with his fifth release 'Wild Side Of Life' (which peaked at number 33) and Quickly retired from the music business a year later.

The Strangers with Mike Shannon

One And One Is Two

The Strangers were a group from Liverpool which boasted Joe Fagin as their vocalist when they appeared alongside The Beatles at early Aintree Institute shows in Liverpool. On the other hand it is possible the band may also have been the outfit which later featured Mike Shannon as their lead singer

While called simply The Strangers they never made or released a record but a group billed as 'The Strangers with Mike Shannon' were on the receiving end of a genuine Lennon/McCartney song.

In January 1964 The Beatles were in Paris and Lennon & McCartney were on a deadline to finish a new song for Billy J Kramer, but Lennon apparently wasn't too happy with the duo's efforts. Talking about their song 'One And One Is Two', he said, "Billy J's career is finished when he gets this song."

It seems that Kramer wasn't impressed either

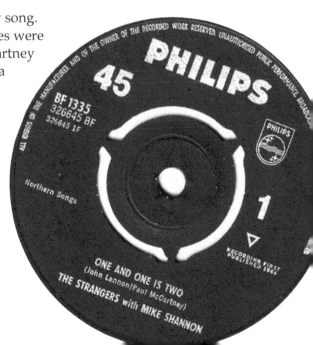

and he turned the song down (and recorded an American song called 'Little Children' instead) as, reportedly, so did The Fourmost, another band managed by Brian Epstein. But The Strangers with Mike Shannon, described by sources as "a British group", did record it and issued it on the Philips label in May 1964 – when it failed to chart.

Doris Troy
Ain't She Cute

American R&B singer Doris Troy was among the backing singers on Billy Preston's first album for The Beatles' Apple label, which was produced by George Harrison and included the hit single 'That's The Way God Planned It'.

As a result the New York-born daughter of a Baptist preacher was quickly signed up to Apple where Harrison produced a song he had co-written with the singer as her debut single. 'Ain't She Cute' was issued in the UK in February 1970 and later in America but it failed to make an impression on either side of the Atlantic.

Troy's one solo album for Apple featured the likes of Harrison, Ringo Starr, Klaus Voormann and Stephen Stills as backing musicians but with no new hits to her name – she had reached the US top ten with 'Just One Look' in 1963 and the UK top forty in 1964 with 'Wathcha Gonna Do About It' – Troy returned to America in 1974. She later appeared in the musical *Mama I Want To Sing*, which was based on her life and was performed in America and in London in 1995. Troy died in February 2004 aged 67.

Beatles' Covers Uncovered

Paul McCartney once said "I've never been annoyed by a cover version." You can only assume he had never heard versions of the songs he once called "his babies" performed by the motley collection of actors, dogs, cartoon characters and oddball instrumentalists who have, over the years, attempted to cash in and grab a headline by

By April 1964 as Beatlemania swept the US they had the top five chart places

recording a Beatles tune. To paraphrase a Beatles song title – some of them should have known better.

Many things have been written about The Beatles over the years. Some it has been deeply profound, some of it has been blatantly scandalous but the great majority of it has been in tribute to the biggest and the arguably the best band of all time.

And while you might want to argue about who is best (and who is biggest) there are certain facts that you can't argue about when it comes to The Beatles.

They have notched up more British number one albums than any other act (15); registered the biggest selling album in the UK (Sgt

Pepper); and released a total of 40 number one albums, singles and EPs – and that's only taking in the US and the UK.

In America they have sold more albums than any other band and also topped the list of Top Selling Hot 100 artists in Billboard's 50 year chart history, published in 2008. They share the accolade of most albums in the chart at the same time (seven) with U2 and The Monkees. In April 1964 they actually held all top five positions in the US singles chart and in the same month also claimed a record-breaking 14 records in the US Hit 100 chart.

And while they are currently one of only two acts to have passed the magic one billion sales mark worldwide – although there's a chance the late Michael Jackson might join them and Elvis Presley on the list – the songs which Lennon & McCartney and Harrison wrote remain among the most coveted and covered compositions in pop history.

But which are the best, the worst, the most bizarre or the most successful of these covers? There are somewhere close to 300 'Beatles' songs to chose from – over 160 credited to the partnership of Lennon/McCartney while Harrison added a host of solo creations alongside a handful of tracks where all four group members were listed as composers – and there aren't many that somebody somewhere hasn't had a go at.

But while we know they couldn't all be classics – never forget 'Octopus's Garden', 'Yellow Submarine', 'Flying' or even 'Maxwell's Silver Hammer' – there were seemingly enough great, good, catchy, reasonable and even oddball creations to attract literally thousands of artists from the worlds of rock and pop, jazz and classical and folk and soul.

The attraction for all musicians has always been the quality of the songs created and performed by The Beatles during their time together. But for rock legend Alice Cooper there was another ingredient in the mix. "There's nothing more fun than getting together with a bunch of guys and just doing Beatles' songs – it's the best thing in the world," says the man who lists 'Bulldog' and 'Back In The USSR' – "we always do that one" – as two tracks he has covered.

But the man who topped the UK charts with 'School's Out' in 1972 warns against covering some others. "There are certain tracks you don't touch. 'A Day In The Life' would be a hard song to try and cover because it is just SO Beatles that you could never do it."

Fellow Beatles fan Graham Gouldman was a member of three-time British chart toppers 1OCC – who also covered Lennon and McCartney compositions – and he has more words of warning for those artists contemplating covering a Beatles song. "If you are going to mess with a Beatles song you'd better be really, really careful with it as far as I'm concerned, but there's nothing wrong with paying homage to The Beatles."

And Simply Red's Mick Hucknall is equally adamant, "Some people are just too good to do covers of." The man with sales of over 40 million records under his belt further explained in 2006, "The Beatles are very difficult because the engineering of their records has been a huge inspiration to what I've been doing recently."

Whether the 25 cover versions I have chosen – a mixture of the most famous, the not so well known, the successful, the surprising, the disappointing and my own favourites – have all been carefully crafted is open to debate but I suspect they were all attempted as some sort of a tribute to the group which set new standards both in terms of record sales and, perhaps more importantly, in the quality of their song writing.

Across The Universe

Despite being covered by only a handful of artists, this is a song that seemingly means more to musicians than fans. Barbara Dickson, 10CC, Fiona Apple, Cilla Black and David Bowie head the short list of artists to cover the third track from the *Let It Be* album.

The Beatles opened with a sliding guitar intro leading into John's ever-so echoey vocals over piano, tom toms, tamboura and sitar. Two girl fans brought in from the street add the high pitch vocal backing alongside a swirling chorus and the whole thing fades out at 3.20 seconds.

In comparison Bowie's 1995 version from his *Young Americans* album features some much affected vocalising over a harder drum and guitar backing and lacks any of the lightness of the original. In fact the 'thin white duke' gets more urgent – and bizarrely more repetitive – as the tracks runs on to a lengthy 4.25 seconds.

Dickson picks the song as her favourite Beatles song – "it's one of the best songs I've ever heard" – and uses it regularly to close her live shows despite what she views as public indifference to the song. "I love the words which are so abstract and transcendental but the public don't like it at all but I don't care about that – I care about what I like to play."

Gouldman, who returned to the road with 10CC in 2009 (and they were still going strong in 2012) recalls that it was

their manager's love of the song which persuaded them to cover it, adding, "When you sing a Beatles song you enter Beatles world." While 10CC stuck to the original arrangement, the song, according to Gouldman, is a combination of "beautiful chords with fantastic lyrics, although I'm not really sure what the hell is going on, but that's not the point – all you need to do is feel."

The song, which Paul admits has a "change the world theme", was also covered by Fiona Apple on the soundtrack to the film *Pleasantville* and her version was voted number four on the Rolling Stone reader's list of Best Beatles Covers. "Usually it's hard for me to sing other people's songs but that one meant something to me", she once told Mojo magazine. "I think it's all wrapped up in the 'nothing's going to change the world' line. It's so powerful."

And I Love Her

There have been literally hundreds of versions of this song which was written by Paul and first appeared on the Beatles' *A Hard Day's Night* album, issued to accompany the release of their first major film.

The fab four perform it as an acoustic track with a guitar intro and Paul's best ballad-style vocal appearing alongside some fine guitar work by George.

Among the long list of cover versions – which ranges from Ken Dodd, Jose Feliciano, The Wailers and Smokey Robinson to Bobby Womack, Connie Francis, Neil Diamond and Julio Iglesias – it's one by Esther Phillips which impressed McCartney. The man whose relationship with Jane Asher inspired him to write the song and who recorded his own live MTV *Unplugged* version in1991, once said, "She changed our 'And I Love Her' to 'And I Love Him' and did a great version of it."

American jazz singer Sarah Vaughan also played the same sex-change trick with the title line on her version which overwhelms the original at least in terms of length

The Beatles' 2.25 seconds original pales against Vaughan's four minute version which starts out with muted brass and bass before the American singer's slow jazz vocal comes in, backed by a chorus of the changed title line And I Love Him. She picks up the pace and brings in some electric guitar and piano plus swirling string effects before ending with a much-repeated title line and some odd scat singing.

For Britain's longest serving pop star Cliff Richard, including the song on his 2001 *Wanted* album was an obvious move. "There's no way I could do an album of covers and ignore The Beatles but I did not want to do anything too obvious", he says while admitting that he had sung 'She Loves You' live but found it a difficult song to change. "'And I Love Her' was a ballad that we could actually change and move around to get a brand new sound – and there is kind of an R&B feel to it."

Can't Buy Me Love

Soul singers Mary Wells and The Supremes and 1960s pop legends Brenda Lee and Jackie DeShannon are alongside acts as diverse as Johnny Rivers, Dwight Yoakham, Dweezil Yappa, The King Singers and an all-girl group called The Korean Kittens – who offered up a version in

English with the chorus in a Korean – on the list of acts who have covered this song which also featured in *A Hard Day's Night*.

The Beatles open with a stirring group chorus as Ringo's pounding drum work leads into Paul's lead vocal. There's some strong chorus work before Paul's scream brings in an accomplished guitar solo from George and the song runs out, after a host of repeated title lines, at just over 2 minutes.

Despite the long list of cover versions – including Peter Sellars and Henry Mancini – it was the first lady of jazz, Ella Fitzgerald, who made the biggest impact.

She begins with a big band intro before laying her unique jazz style all over the song. With the band running along at a pace, Miss F hits the high notes and indulges in some free-form jazz singing before the whole thing winds up with a big band and vocal finale after 2.33 seconds.

Fitzgerald, who died in 1996, made the UK top 40 in April 1964 and her version remains on record as the first cover version of a Beatles hit to ever reach the charts … and she also impressed both a Beatle and their producer. "When somebody like Ella Fitzgerald sang 'Can't Buy Me Love' it gave them (The Beatles) an almost royal seal of approval", was George Martin's view while Paul just said, "Ella Fitzgerald did a version of it which I was very honoured by."

Come Together

For many people this was the stand out track on the Beatles' *Abbey Road* album and it certainly found favour with a host of artists from a wide (and occasionally bizarre) range of musical genres including Ike and Tina Turner, Diana Ross, Meat Loaf, Howard Jones, James Last, Desmond Dekker, Dionne Warwick and The Butthole Surfers.

They were all influenced by the song that begins with bass and drums and the memorable 'schh' intro before pounding drums, together with some powerful bass and guitar work, help build the emotion. John adopts an abbreviated vocal style before George's highly effective guitar work links with the drum and vocal chorus passages.

George Martin, producer of the original Beatles version, was recruited to create Aerosmith's standout cover from the less than successful 1978 *Sgt Pepper* film soundtrack which hit the US top 30 and was voted number 5 on the Rolling Stone readers' list of Best Beatle Covers.

Thirteen years later the multi-million selling US rock band performed the song again as part of a Grammy Award show tribute to John Lennon.

Amid audience applause and a ringing guitar, Steve Tyler declares, "John, this is for you." From then on Aerosmith set off to produce a thumping heavyweight version with blistering guitar work and grating vocals creating a powerful but faithful cover.

After Michael Jackson – who had bought the rights to virtually all the Lennon & McCartney compositions including this one in 1984 for $47 million – pitched up with a top three hit version in 1992, the song went back into the UK top 20 in 1995 with a charity version in aid of War Child from the Smokin' Mojo Filters which featured Noel Gallagher, Paul Weller and Paul McCartney.

Day Tripper

As one side of The Beatles double A-side single – alongside 'We Can Work It Out' – this song raced to number one in December 1965.

It arrives with the unmistakeable and unforgettable bass intro from Paul to accompany his own slightly strained but effective vocal which he shares with John's gruffer contribution and George's solo guitar work.

One of the many acts to cover 'Day Tripper' was an artist who was among the first signings to The Beatles' Apple record label in 1968 where he released his debut album.

James Taylor offers a version with strings and drums behind his slightly drawled vocal work. Faster and more urgent than the original with some odd falsetto moments plus lengthy guitar breaks, Taylor conjures up a rock track rather a pop song.

Talking some years later, Taylor looked back on his 1979 version from his hit album *Flag* and explained that it was "just one of those things when we had time at the end of a day and somebody started playing a groove and before you know it, it's a track."

Otis Redding took the song into the UK top 50 in March 1976 while Jimi Hendrix included it as part of an early BBC radio session and the assorted list of cover versions runs from Rod Stewart, The Flamin' Groovies, Cheap Trick, Whitesnake and Julian Lennon to Lulu, Nancy Sinatra, Ann Murray, Sandie Shaw and Sandy Nelson plus, perhaps most oddly, one from Mae West.

From Me To You

The song that finally brought The Beatles a number one hit in the UK was less successful in America where it peaked outside the

Top 100. While it's a song that boasts few cover versions – The Crickets and Mae West both included it on albums – it has been featured in Christmas TV advertising campaigns by both the US store Macy's and Britain's own John Lewis.

The Beatles open with a group intro before Lennon's vocals take over the lead although he struggles on the falsetto parts. His inserts a brief harmonica break midway and the song continues to a repeated To You, To You, To You plus harmonica and striking guitar note ending at 1.52secs.

The most significant cover version came from American singer Del Shannon who supported The Beatles at London's Royal Albert Hall in May 1963 where he heard them sing the song – and was suitably impressed. "No one had heard of The Beatles here (in the US) but I knew they were great writers so I just picked up on one of their songs," said the singer who committed suicide in 1990.

His version follows much the same pattern as The Beatles as far as the arrangement but Shannon is more at home with the falsetto parts – it was a feature on many of his hits – but adopts a lower register for the bulk of his vocals. There's a tinnier drum sound throughout but with no harmonica break or ending, the song finishes with a Da Da Da Da Dum Dum fade out at a slightly longer 1.58 seconds.

Released in June 1963, Shannon's version reached number 77 in the US charts and earned Lennon and McCartney their first American hit as song writers.

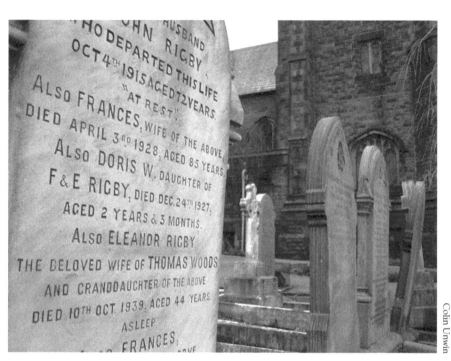

Colin Unwin

Eleanor Rigby

This classic Beatles song was written by Paul and boasts more than 300 cover versions including efforts from folk singers, jazzers, crooners, soul singers, rockers – and an English politician.

Joan Baez, Stanley Jordon, Sarah Vaughan – who made a entire album of Beatles' songs – Paul Anka, Frankie Valli, The Supremes, Jackie Wilson, Richie Havens, Booker T, The Four Tops, Vanilla Fudge and Rick Wakeman are among the main contenders ... plus an effort in Latin by Derek Enright, the former Labour MP for Hemsworth.

On their *Revolver* album, the Beatles open the two minute track with a group chorus over a double string quartet leading into Paul's classic up tempo but still slightly melancholy vocal.

On the back of Ray Charles' 1968 US and UK top 40 hit version, fellow American soul superstar Aretha Franklin went top 20 in the US in December 1969 with her version.

It opens with jazz piano leading a first person vocal with the strange sounding line 'I'm Eleanor Rigby' and some funky drum work. Faster and more soulful but with less of a pleading vocal than the original, it features an electric piano break, girly chorus and some screaming vocals as it runs on to over 2.30 seconds.

Get Back

This was among the set of songs The Beatles performed live on the roof of their Savile Row offices in January 1969 and the one that closed *Let It Be,* the last studio album released by The Beatles.

With Paul taking the lead – after John's unscripted opening parody of 'sweet Loretta fart' – the song offers up an insistent bass and heavy drum beat with George's sweeter guitar breaks adding to the mix. Billy Preston throws in some funky piano which leads into Paul's more urgent vocal and finally a smattering of applause from the crowd on the roof.

In contrast soul star Al Green brings his extraordinary voice to the song with a big band backing featuring heavy brass interludes and a much heavier guitar break. The whole thing pounds along with Green's unique

vocal urging.

While Rod Stewart's version from the film *All This And World War II* reached number 11 in the UK in December 1976, Ike and Tina Turner, Amen Corner, Elton John, Doris Troy and Status Quo all gave 'Get Back' a go.

Got To Get You Into My Life

The song Paul once admitted was "an ode to dope" brought two very different acts top ten hits on opposite sides of the Atlantic and in different decades.

While French star Johnny Hallyday, the glorious twosome Sonny & Cher and groups Blood Sweat & Tears and The Four Tops all recorded the song, it was extravagant American funk/soul outfit Earth Wind & Fire and hard-working British soul band Cliff Bennett and the Rebel Rousers who made the biggest impact.

Alice Cooper was moved to highlight Earth Wind & Fire's 1978 US top ten and UK top 40 hit version, from the Sgt Pepper film soundtrack, as "a really good cover" and readers of Rolling Stone agreed as they voted it number seven on the list of Best Beatle Covers.

The Beatles 1966 offering on *Revolver* is Paul's Tamla Motown inspired moment which introduces a brass section on a Beatles record for the first time. They work alongside Martin's Hammond organ while Paul's lead vocal is answered by John and George, who also contributes a striking guitar solo.

Cliff Bennett sticks with the same brass section intro while his early harsh vocal work gets easier as things go along. The chopping brass mixes with the backing vocals and Chas Hodges – later of Chas & Dave fame – contributes a short but funky piano break.

Part of Beatles manager Brian Epstein's growing stable of artists in the mid sixties, Cliff Bennett and his band peaked at number six in the

UK in August 1966, the same month as The Beatles released the chart topping *Revolver* album containing their original version.

A Hard Day's Night

The title song to the Beatles' first feature film – which was created in a matter of days by John and Paul after Ringo had coined the phrase 'it's been a hard day's night' and seen it adopted as the film's title – has had quite a few takers when it comes to cover versions.

The original opens with George's memorable strident guitar chord which leads into John taking lead and Paul offering backing vocals alongside bongos and Martin's piano work. George's guitar work stands out as a mid-song break and the whole thing fades to an end after 2.29 seconds.

The most successful – and one of the shortest – cover versions came from actor and comedian Peter Sellars whose work with the Goons made him a hero to The Beatles. His extraordinary effort, lasting just 1 minute and 43 seconds, made it to number 14 in December 1965.

After opening with mediaeval period music Sellars launches into his full-on impersonation of actor Laurence Olivier in *Richard III* mode and talks his way slowly through the affair, putting emphasis on the story line of the song. More appropriate mood music takes him into a truly menacing second verse.

Sellars was invited to perform the song as Richard III seated on a throne on a December 1965 Granada TV show entitled *The Music Of Lennon And McCartney* and Paul recalled it fondly. "He did a very funny impression of Larry Olivier doing 'A Hard Day's Night'."

Less successful were versions from Ramsey Lewis – a top 30 US hit – The Supremes, Otis Redding, Billy Preston, Dionne Warwick, Peggy Lee, Chet Atkins and, not forgetting, either Mr Sing-along Max Bygraves and piano wonder-woman Mrs Mills.

Help!

Credited as the first Beatles song ever to be covered and used in a TV commercial – by the Ford Motor Co in 1985 for a reputed $100,000 fee – the original version by the fab four was the title track of their fifth album and second feature film made in 1965.

The Beatles open with a pleading vocal from the composer John which leads into a pacy track with some big guitar notes from George alongside distinctive side breaks. It runs to an end after 2.18 seconds with John's meaningful double 'help me' line.

For Tina Turner, the song represented the second hit record of her newly resurrected solo career in 1984 and brought her a deserved UK top 40 hit.

She comes in over a simple piano with an emotion charged vocal. The focus is on her voice and the supporting piano, while muted drums lead into a chorus and sax solo before she launches into a slightly over the top vocal and a long single note ending on 4.28 seconds.

While punk band The Damned featured the song as the B-side of 'New Rose' in October 1976 – considered to be the first ever punk release – the likes of Dolly Parton, Deep Purple, Alma Cogan and The Carpenters all offered up their own versions but the biggest hit came from Banarama and the spoof group La Na Nee Noo Noo (featuring Dawn French, Jennifer Saunders and Kathy Burke), who hit number three in Mach 1989 in aid of Comic Relief.

And not content with his version of his Shakespearean-style 'A Hard Day's Night', Peter Sellars returned to perform this one as a vicar giving a sermon complete with full angelic choir backing.

Here Comes The Sun

Six years after the split up of The Beatles and seven years after the song appeared on the band's *Abbey Road* album, George's song was taken into the top ten by Steve Harley and Cockney Rebel.

The original version was made in 1969 by just three Beatles as John was still recovering after a car crash and George starts things off with his gentle guitar picking and double tracked vocal. The easy up-beat feel is maintained thanks to some effective drum and guitar work plus handclapping and harmonium and breezy backing vocals from George and Paul.

Busy recording his *Love's A Prima Donna* album, Harley turned to the song when he found himself one track short. "I said I was going to do a cover of 'Here Comes The Sun' which I had done acoustically in folk clubs. I adored the simplicity of it and am something of a romantic but I saw the whole thing as more apocalyptic than George's up beat version and went for that sort of staccato accent."

He sets the song rolling with the same building guitar/drum intro as the original but gives it a harder feel with sharp breaks and chorus work. His unique take on the vocals gives the song a less up-beat feel as it runs out with lots of 'it's alright' into a growing chorus and a backing which stops abruptly on a single bell.

Warned that it was "madness" to try and cover a Beatles classics, Harley delivered his version and recalls fondly that "EMI loved it when I presented it to them and it was such a dangerous move, that it went to number ten in the charts."

American singer Richie Havens also charted with the song in May 1971 – it was to be his first and only top 20 hit – while Nina Simone, Hugo Montenegro and Sandy Farina, from the *Sgt Pepper* movie, all picked on George's classic summer anthem.

Hey Jude

The list of artists who have covered Paul's song – which The
Beatles took to number one in September 1968 – is estimated to run
close to a thousand and people are still counting.

Wilson Pickett leads the pack with his UK top 20 and US top
30 hit from 1969 which he recorded at Muscle Shoals studio at the
suggestion of Duane Allman, who ended up playing guitar on the
version which was voted number 9 on Rolling Stone's readers' list
of Best Beatle Covers.

He's joined on the list of cover artists by the likes of King
Curtis, Petula Clark, The Everly Brothers, Dionne Warwick, Count
Basie, Bing Crosby, Chet Atkins, Ella Fitzgerald, The New Christy
Minstrels, The Ray Charles Singers – without Ray Charles – and
Greek superstar Nana Mouskouri …complete with a bouzouki
solo.

Paul opens up the original with a simple vocal and piano intro
followed by percussion and a group chorus   as
the whole thing builds into the most
insistent pounding and at
times frenzied four minute run
down of any track, featuring 36
instruments, repeated chorus
and solo vocal/screams
plus some background
chatting, before running
out of steam after seven
minutes.

On their version from
the 1969 album *Puzzle
People*, Motown favourites
the Temptations follow an

odd route.

They begin with a jazzy piano intro and fuzz guitar at double time before the slow lead vocal comes in over a mix of falsetto choruses and the occasional deep bass line. The group members swap vocals in an uncoordinated fashion as they attempt (and

fail) to build up to the same frenzied ending after just 3.30 seconds.

This was also a song that leading instrumental group – and five times UK single chart toppers – The Shadows featured on their 1986 top ten album *Moonlight Shadows*. And according to long-time group member Bruce Welch it all came about because of questions asked by their record company.

"They did market research where they went out with a list of 40 songs and asked people what songs they would like to hear The Shadows play. We would then have a long short list of about 25 tracks and decide what we wanted to do", he explains before pointing out the one essential ingredient in the mix. "It was always important that Hank (Marvin) could get a performance out of it on the guitar. As an instrumental band, the melodies have to be really interesting and Hank has to get some feeling for the song."

I Am The Walrus

"John's baby, a great one" was Paul's view of this song while ex-Sex Pistol Glen Matlock simply says "now, that is wacky."

There we have two interesting assessments of the stand-out track from the ground-breaking *Magical Mystery Tour* EP and television show The Beatles created for Christmas 1967 which was described by the TV critic of the Daily Express as "blatant rubbish."

Banned by the BBC because the band sang the word 'knickers', the song was a favourite of its creator. "It's one of those that has enough little bitties going to keep you interested even a hundred years later," said John who also took credit for including a live radio broadcast in the original version because "it was interesting to mix the whole thing with a live radio coming through it."

The original, lasting over 4.30 seconds, mixes all the usual instruments plus electric piano and mellotron over heavy drums and bass lines which lead into John's urgent and passionate lead vocal. It gets weirder as it goes along with the excerpt from *King Lear*, broadcast on the BBC Third Programme, pitched in alongside the 16 male and female voices of the Mike Sammes Singers.

It's a song that, perhaps understandably, has not attracted too many cover versions but British progressive rock band Spooky Tooth gave it a go in 1970 on their final *The Last Puff* album

They give the whole

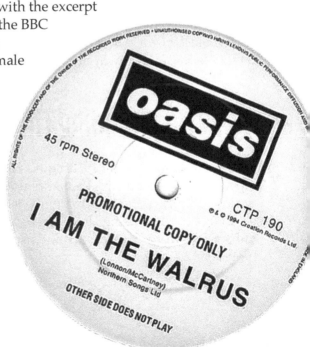

thing a much heavier feel as they open up with a significantly slower rendition featuring the much harder and more menacing vocals of Mike Harrison and some ultra long drum and guitar breaks. More urgent and less fun than the original, it builds to a heavy climax after 6.20 seconds.

In January 1996 Oasis included a live version on their US top ten *Wonderwall* release which was voted number 2 on the Rolling Stone list of readers' Best Beatle Covers (losing out to U2's version of Helter Skelter) while Styx offered up a version as have Lol Coxhill, Frank Zappa, John Otway and Men Without Hats.

I Saw Her Standing There

Recorded for their debut 1963 album *Please Please Me*, the Beatles open their recording with Paul's scene-setting 'live' count in to this fast-paced rocker. Paul carries off the lead vocal work with the band pushing the whole thing along at a pace. They throw in some screams, nifty early George guitar work and handclaps to go out on a single note after 2.52 seconds.

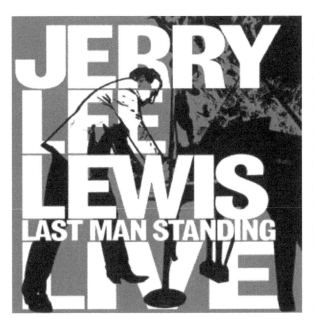

Among the pretty substantial list of artists who have covered the song which featured in The Beatles' live set from 1962 onwards are two artists whose own recordings influenced the group in their earliest years – American rock icons Jerry Lee Lewis and Little Richard.

They joined forces in 2006 on Lewis's *Last Man Standing* album to record a fast country tinged rock version which opens with 'the Killer's' echo-laden drawled count in. The track also features some effective piano playing from Lee and trademark screams from Richard with Lee taking the lead and Richard coming in to share the vocals and bring his piano to the fore alongside some nifty guitar work. They team up for a shared piano spot which brings it all to an end after 2.20 seconds.

140 From Me To You

At New York's Madison Square Garden in November 1974 Elton John was joined on stage by John Lennon – making what would be his last ever live concert appearance – and they offered up a unique version of the song which became a UK top 40 hit in March 1981 and the B-side of John's 'Philadelphia Freedom' single in America.

Speaking about the concert experience Elton recalled how the song was chosen, saying "I thought of 'I Saw Her Standing There'. And he (John) had never sung it. It was McCartney who sang it. John was so knocked out because he'd never actually sung the lead before."

Perhaps less impressive was teenage sensation Tiffany's version which appeared in June 1988 as 'I Saw Him Standing There' and hit the top ten in both the UK and US, while in 2008 The Supremes version recorded for their bizarre 1964 *A Little Bit Of Liverpool* album was finally issued. Others on the list of covers include Jerry Garcia, Maggie Bell and Hank Williams Jnr, alongside Johnny Hallyday's French version and one from The Pete Best Band, led by the Beatles' original drummer who was unceremoniously replaced by Ringo in 1962.

In My Life

Considered by some to be John's answer to Paul's 'Yesterday' which was written a few months earlier, this hugely autobiographical song took on an added extra and hugely emotional dimension when country legend Johnny Cash covered it in 2002.

The Beatles version on *Revolver* uses a simple guitar behind John's poignant vocal work while Paul offers vocal support. Ringo keeps time throughout on drums and tambourine while Martin adds in his speeded-up piano section.

Cash, who died a year after his recording was made, featured the track on his acclaimed *American IV: The Man Comes Around* album produced by Rick Rubin.

The 'man in black' comes up with a extraordinary moving version which replicates the feel of the original but features an almost painful vocal performance plus double harmonium and orchestra bells. Running to 2.54 seconds – 30 seconds longer than the original – the song closes with repeated titles and the same easy guitar style.

Recorded at Cash's own Cabin Studio in Nashville, readers of Rolling Stone voted the version number 10 on their list of Best Beatle Covers, ahead of efforts from a star-studded list including Rod Stewart, Judy Collins, Jose Feliciano, Stephen Stills, Lena Horne, Keith Moon, Don Williams, Bette Midler, Mary Hopkin, The Dave Matthews Band and jazz violinist Stephane Grappelli.

Let It Be

This is the title track from The Beatles' final studio album which was begun in 1969 – before the *Abbey Road* album – but eventually released in May 1970 after Abbey Road.

Legendary producer Phil Spector joined the party in March 1970 to rework the abandoned *Get Back* album project into *Let It Be*, much to the anger of Paul who cited his involvement during his action to dissolve The Beatles partnership, which he launched in December 1970.

According to regular producer Martin, Paul was "particularly upset" with Spector's treatment of 'The Long Winding Road' and 'Let It Be', to which he added tape echo while also editing and overdubbing verses and solos from different takes.

What ends up on the record came from the very last day The Beatles ever recorded together – on January 4 1970 – and it opens with just piano and Paul's voice for the first minute before drums come in ahead of a brass section, Billy Preston's organ and George's blistering guitar solo. A soulful Paul takes it on over more guitar work to end on four minutes with cellos and an extended single piano note.

The most successful cover version came from the 1987 charity record for Ferry Aid which went to number one thanks to vocal support from the likes of Paul McCartney, Mark Knopfler, Gary Moore, Andy Bell and Kate Bush, while American blind soul singer Clarence Carter, who hit the charts with Patches in 1970, also gave it his best shot.

He chooses to open with a heavenly choir and while he keeps much the same feel as the original he slows it down to highlight his almost spoken deep gravel voice. Things speed up as choir and organ and guitar recreate 'The Beatles' sound before Carter reverts to talking his way through to the end on 3.25 seconds when brass, choir, and organ get behind his big vocal finish.

Among the other artists who have recorded the song are Dion, The Persuasions, Gladys Knight, Joe Cocker, Bill Withers, John Denver, Meat Loaf, Ike & Tina Turner and Richie Havens, but strangely folk singer Joan Baez has the only other chart version – she peaked at number 49 in the US in November 1971.

Lucy In The Sky With Diamonds

Inspired by John's and Paul's love of Lewis Carroll's *Alice In Wonderland* stories – "in our mind it was an Alice thing which both of us loved", said Paul – this song courted controversy from the day it was first released as part of The Beatles' *Sgt Pepper's Lonely Hearts Club Band* album in June 1967.

By taking the letters LSD from the title words, many people assumed the song was about drugs rather than the drawing four year old Julian Lennon had done at nursery and named 'Lucy In The Sky With Diamonds' The assumptions annoyed The Beatles as John once recounted, "I saw Mel

Torme introducing a
Lennon-McCartney
show, saying how
'Lucy In the Sky With
Diamonds' was about
LSD. It never was and
nobody believes me."

Whatever it was
about, The Beatles
version features Paul
on Hammond organ
behind John's double
tracked voice coupled
with Paul's harmony
and George's fuzzed
guitar and a droning
tamboura. It builds
over Ringo's drums and moves along eerily at times on a repeated
title chorus to end at 3.23 seconds.

U2's Bono and The Edge offered up a version from the 2007
soundtrack to the film *Across The Universe* which featured covers of 33
Beatles songs.

They open with a slow building keyboard before Bono's vocal leads
into a string break. While the vocal is less distorted than the original
and features the same drum patterns and big chorus, the whole thing
has a powerful feel with slow gentle passages plus swirling distorted
backing and a gradual fade out at a lengthy 4.18 seconds.

Elton John's version featuring John Lennon topped the US chart in
January 1975 after hitting the UK top ten in December 1974 and was
voted in at number 12 on the Rolling Stone list of Best Beatle Covers.

While Katie Melua offered up a live rendition in 2005 and Noel
Harrison, Natalie Cole and comedian Bill Murray recorded their own
versions, it was *Star Trek's* very own Captain Kirk who made most

headlines. Actor William Shatner included his spoken word effort on his album *The Transformed Man* and later recognised what he had done when he admitted, "Some people believe my version of Lucy in the Sky is the worst musical rendition of all time."

Michelle

This song came to the attention of producer and songwriter Tony Hatch when the Beatles' music publisher Dick James played it to him even before the group's *Rubber Soul* album had been released in December 1965.

"I don't think he was supposed to look for cover versions of songs before The Beatles' versions came out," recalls the man who wrote hits for The Searchers ('Sugar And Spice' under the name Fred Nightingale), Petula Clark, Scott Walker and his song writing partner Jackie Trent.

What Hatch heard that day was The Beatles with a relaxed guitar intro into Paul's vocal over drums and guitar and with a little bit of French thrown in as Paul's plaintive 'I love you' and 'I need you' lines are repeated over a gentle guitar and bass backing.

After picking out 'Michelle' as a song most likely to succeed, Hatch was slipped an advance copy of the album and went off to record his version with the folk trio

The Overlanders.

Laurie Mason, Paul Arnold and Pete Bartholomew opt for a louder guitar intro than the original and the three part harmony is also more forceful. Played at a slightly faster tempo but with the same 'French' breaks they come to a halt a little sooner after 2.20 seconds.

Composer Paul explained the inclusion of French lyrics in the song which won the Grammy for Best Song in1967 by saying simply that it "always sounded like a French thing", while singer Steve Harley describes it as "a seriously great song which is much more complicated than it seems and a difficult song to play and to learn."

While The Overlanders went to number one in January 1966 – it was their one and only hit – producer Hatch was aware that there was another issue at stake. "I think the worst crime was for Dick to get another cover version on something that was already scheduled within EMI."

The company which oversaw The Beatles' recordings did indeed have another cover version all set to go, but David and Jonathan (singers/composers Roger Cook and Roger Greenaway) peaked at number 11 in the UK and reached the US top 20 with their effort.

Among the more than 700 reported covers of Michelle there have been efforts from surfers Jan and Dean, The Four Tops, Johnny Mathis, Booker T, Andy Williams, The Sandpipers, The Bachelors, The Lettermen and TV actor David McCallum, star of The Man From Uncle and, more recently, NCIS.

Ob-La-Di-Ob-La-Da

The inspiration for this song from the 1968 album *The Beatles* (dubbed *The White Album*) came from a Nigerian bongo player who used the phrase when he was around the Beatles. Jimmy Scott explained that it meant "life goes on" and from there Paul was inspired to create his

most catchy singalong track

The original starts out with a child-like piano opening with hand claps that lead into Paul's reggae-inspired vocal with John and George offering back-up before chugging saxes, a piccolo and Scott himself on bongos join in to take the whole thing to a slightly confused ending after just over 3 minutes.

The band who had most success with a cover was Scottish group Marmalade who notched up a total of eight UK top ten hits between 1968 and 1976 but none bigger than this version.

They opt to go straight into Dean Ford's vocal – which at times sounds remarkably like Paul's – with a big brass backing and thumping piano. They make it a slightly shorter, much simpler and more straightforward pop song with brass and piano breaks.

Ford, Junior Campbell, Pat Fairlie, Graham Knight and Alan Whitehead went to number one in the UK in December 1968, while The Bedrocks hit the UK top 20 at the same time with a rival cover while versions also came along from Arthur Conley, Johnny Mathis and The Boston Pops Orchestra.

She's Leaving Home

Paul's most plaintive track from the *Sgt Pepper* album has a unique claim in Beatles' history as the only song on which none of the group actually played any instruments.

The original version features a string section of four violins, two violas, two

cellos, a double bass and a harp (played by Sheila Bromberg, the first woman ever to appear on a Beatles' recording) which actually opens the track before Paul's vocal. Rising strings come in but it remains a simple slow song as Paul hits some high notes and John adds his emotion laden 'bye byes' before the strings take over and bring it to an end after 3.34 seconds.

Harry Nilsson was perhaps closest to John – they were together during some of the ex-Beatle's most notorious US drinking sessions in the early 1970s and worked together on the US singer's *Pussy Cats* album – but he chose to cover Paul's ballad on his earlier 1968 *Pandemonium Shadow Show* album.

The man John declared as his favourite US singer opens his version with just a piano which runs into a brass backing behind his distinctive vocal. It all becomes much bigger with a louder double tracked vocal coupled with brass and an insistent drum beat before fading to an end after 3.17 seconds.

Having charted with Michelle, David & Jonathan gave it another go with this song but failed to chart while Stevie Wonder's wife Syretta, Bryan Ferry, Al Jarreau and The Royal Philharmonic Orchestra all offered up versions. The one big success was a version by Billy Bragg, with Cara Tivey, which reached number one in May 1988 in support of the charity Child Line.

Something

The first Beatles' hit single not to be written by either John or Paul came from George in 1969. It appeared on the album *Abbey Road* and while it peaked at number four in the UK, it reached number in one America and was described by its creator as "probably the nicest melody I've ever written."

The group's version has a pounding drum intro and some familiar guitar work from George who offers up a slightly strained vocal. With a big string section it builds to an emotional vocal and guitar break and ends after 2.58 seconds with the orchestra and Billy Preston's piano to the fore.

When he wrote the song, it seems that George had Ray Charles in mind but Frank Sinatra got to it first and in 1970 released it as a single which failed to chart on either side of the Atlantic.

He records the song with a woodwind intro over strings and muted brass section which leads into the familiar Sinatra vocal with its slightly odd phrasing. It doesn't build emotionally but just gets louder thanks to the full orchestra and raised vocal and ends on 3.30 seconds after a bizarre big band finale filters away into strings and a final vocal.

Although Charles did

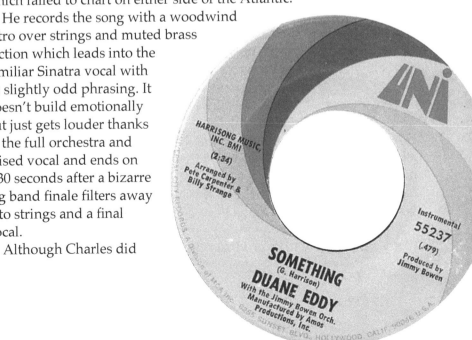

eventually cover the song in 1971, George was less than impressed with 'Old Blue Eyes' decision to record a version. "I wasn't particularly thrilled that Sinatra did 'Something'. I was more interested when Smokey Robinson did it or when James Brown did it," he said.

George was also probably less than impressed with at least part of Sinatra's introduction to the song during his live concerts. While he acknowledged it as "the greatest love song of the past 50 years", he was in the habit of crediting it on stage to Lennon and McCartney.

Joe Cocker was given a preview of the song before the *Abbey Road* album came out and recounts that his reaction to being played George's solo composition was to announce,

"We'll take that one George, it's a killer" and then include it on his 1969 *Joe Cocker* album.

'Something' now stands as probably the second most covered of all Beatles' songs with literally hundreds – maybe even a thousand or more – recorded versions out there, including Shirley Bassey's UK top five hit from June 1970 when she was inspired by seeing Peggy Lee perform the song on the *Ed Sullivan TV show*.

"I just caught the end of Peggy's performance. I was knocked out of my mind. I have to record that number I told myself", the Welsh songstress explained and, despite being warned not to take on The Beatles, she persisted. "The more they told me not to do it, the more I wanted to ... and I proved them wrong."

Alongside these efforts there have been covers by the likes of Martha Reeves, Jim Reeves, Tony Bennett, Booker T, Perry Como, Bill Medley, Sonny & Cher, Liberace, Duane Eddy, Telly Savalas, Engelbert Humperdinck and not forgetting Elvis who included George's masterpiece in his *Aloha From Hawaii* 1973 TV special.

We Can Work It Out

Scottish singer Barbara Dickson, who released a collection of Beatles' songs on *Nothing's Gonna Change My World* in 2006, recalls this song from her earliest days as a performer. "I used to sing 'We Can Work It Out' when I was in a folk group with Rab Noakes and Archie Fisher. It was never really revolutionary to sing their songs in folk clubs", says the woman who later found fame in a Beatles-inspired stage musical.

The group's original version was released as a double A-side single with 'Day Tripper' in 1965 and features Paul as the lead vocalist and an assortment of instruments including tambourine and harmonium. Set at medium pace, it also features an effective blending of vocals from John and Paul before the harmonium brings it all to an end on 2.13 seconds.

Soul legend Stevie Wonder chose this track as the one and only Beatles song he put on record when he included it on the album *Signed, Sealed, Delivered, I'm Yours* in 1971.

He works in a funky keyboard from the outset which leads into his solo vocal and a big backing chorus. It gets more soulful in the second half when he introduces an effective mouth organ break before a final extended soulful falsetto ending at 3.12 seconds.

Released as a single, this cover reached the top 20 in the US and top 30 in the UK. It also earned Wonder a Grammy nomination and sits alongside other efforts from the likes of The Four Seasons, Chaka Khan, Melanie, Deep Purple, Chris Farlowe, The Dillards and Petula Clark and an anonymous version which featured in British TV adverts for Hewlett Packard computers in 1986.

With A Little Help From My Friends

This song segued from the opening title track on *Sgt Pepper* and features probably Ringo's best ever vocal effort, although he had some reservations about the original lyrics written by John and Paul which included the line 'would you throw a tomato at me'.

"I said I am not singing throw a damn tomato at me. I was not going to open myself to being thrown at so we changed that line to walk out on me", recalls Ringo who starts the original track with his vocal and some fine drum work while George Martin adds Hammond organ, Paul plays piano and John adds the cowbell.

The Beatles never intended their version to be a single – Paul described it as "John and I doing a work song for Ringo" – so it fell to former Sheffield steel worker Joe Cocker to make it an international hit with his 1968 version.

His effort builds from a slow organ intro to take in pounding drums and some stinging guitar before Cocker's extraordinary slow pleading vocal comes in over almost no backing at all. It grows and fades with a girl chorus as it develops into a heavier rock ballad than the original with the lead vocal, chorus and a powerful guitar running it out on five minutes.

Cocker, whose flailing hand movements and facial contortions got him into trouble with US TV shows which made him appear behind girl dancers, recounted how he first decided to record The Beatles' song while sitting on the outside toilet of his parent's home. "For some reason it just flashed in my mind", he said and added that he had earlier heard a version by a local band but "I wanted to slow it down and do it waltz time."

With pre-Led Zeppelin man Jimmy Page on guitar, Procol Harum's BJ Wilson on drums and Stevie Winwood on piano, his version reached number one in the UK in November 1968 but failed to crack the US top 60, although his version did get the number three spot on the Rolling Stone readers' list of Best Beatle Covers.

When she was in Willy Russell's 1973 stage musical *John, Paul, George, Ringo And Bert*, Barbara Dickson found herself faced with the job of performing the song at a particularly sensitive time in the story. "It was the most challenging song to work into the show dramatically. After Pete Best had been fired I had to come in with the song so I decided to put it into triplets just as Joe Cocker did it – I felt it was more soulful that way."

Cockney singer Joe Brown was another artist to cover Ringo's best effort and he looks back on it with some regret. "It wasn't

a good idea because unless you do it so different, you could never better what they (The Beatles) did themselves. You could only try to record them in your own way and try to get them out before the Beatles did," is his best advice.

The song was destined to take the UK top spot on two more occasions thanks to Wet Wet Wet in 1988 (it was coupled with Billy Bragg's 'She's Leaving Home' in aid of Child Line) and Sam & Mark in February 2004, while the duo Young Idea hit the top ten in June 1967. This was followed by versions from Ike & Tina Turner, Barbara Streisand, Bon Jovi, ELO, Razorlight, Sham 69 and Pete Frampton from the Sgt Pepper soundtrack while the song also found its way into TV adverts for Gateway computers.

Yesterday

This composition is carved into popular music history as the song with the most recorded versions to its credit. The total number is currently put at over 3000 (and still rising) but that probably wasn't anything Paul had in mind when he first began working on the song in 1963.

Famously given the working title 'Scrambled Eggs', the song evolved over the years until it finally appeared on the Beatles *Help!* album in 1965 as the first solo effort by any member of the group.

Paul was the only one of The Beatles to perform on his song (although George was in the studio at the same time,) which opens with him playing acoustic guitar and runs into his effortless and emotive vocal before a string quartet helps build the song into s simple but classic pop ballad which ends on a series of hmmms at just over two minutes.

Ray Charles was a genuine musical hero to The Beatles but even though they regularly played his songs on stage they never included any on their albums. Nevertheless when he hit the US top 30 and UK top 50 in December 1967 with his version of this song they sent him a congratulatory message saying, "Ray Charles' genius goes on and on. We love you heart and soul."

The 'genius' who was Charles opts for a piano opening to his version which has a slower and darker vocal but continues

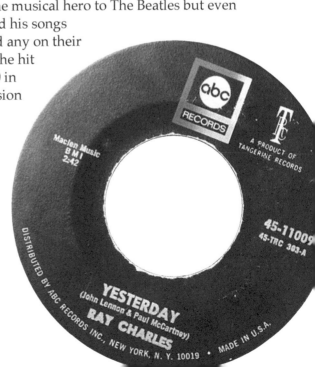

with the strings. His voice rises and falls as we hear the famous "Yesshterday" for the first time while a piano leads into a full orchestra and brass section break. He opts for the same hmmming end with strings and piano after 2.44 seconds.

The song is ranked third on the Broadcast Music Incorporated list of most performed songs on American radio and television with over seven million performances – it lags behind 'Never My Love' and 'You've Lost That Loving Feelin'' – but failed to win a Grammy in 1966 when Herb Alpert's version of 'A Taste Of Honey' (covered by The Beatles on their first album) took Record of the Year, and 'Shadow Of Your Smile' by Tony Bennett was voted Song of the Year.

While Paul admits 'Yesterday' was his "most successful song" and acknowledges that "it just came to me in a dream", John had to accept the plaudits as joint composer despite contributing nothing to the song. "I have had so much accolades for 'Yesterday'. That's Paul's song and Paul's baby. Well done. Beautiful. And I never wished I'd written it."

For Sex Pistol Glen Matlock it represents "a well done bit of schmaltz", while Bob Dylan was seemingly less than impressed with the song. "If you go into the Library of Congress you can find a lot better than that. There are millions of songs like 'Michelle' and 'Yesterday' written in Tin Pan Alley", he once said although he has apparently recorded a version of 'Yesterday' which remains officially unreleased but can be found on the internet.

One man who played a role in the creation of the song was The Shadows' Bruce Welch who lent Paul his villa in Portugal for a holiday in 1965. Before he returned to London, Welch also handed over to Paul the only guitar he had in the house. "He got out of the car and said 'have you got a guitar?' He had this piece of A4 paper with various lyrics scribbled on it and he played me a thing he called 'Scrambled Eggs' on my guitar. If I hadn't had a guitar there, I wouldn't have got to hear 'Yesterday' that day," he says.

Oddly The Shadows never did record the song on any of their collections of popular tunes – "it was probably a bit hackneyed at the time and recorded too often", says Welch.

Chris Farlowe is another who chose not to record the song although he was one of the first to be offered it. Paul had reportedly asked Billy J Kramer if he wanted to record the song and when he said no, the Beatle turned to the British singer who would reach number one in 1966 with the Jagger/Richards song 'Out Of Time'.

Paul had apparently left a demo of the song with Farlowe's mother but the singer was still not persuaded to record it and declared "I don't like it. It's not for me. It's too soft. I need a good rocker."

Despite the huge number of covers only one version of the song has ever made it into the UK top ten and that came from

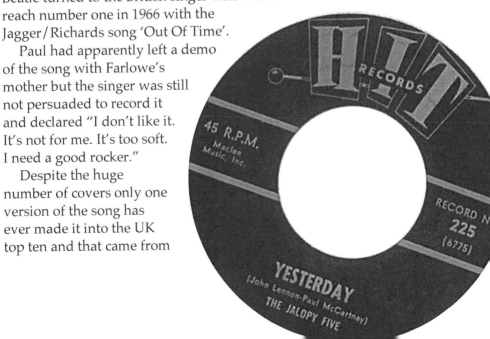

158 From Me To You

Matt Monro in October 1965. His number eight hit was also produced by George Martin, who once christened the ex-London bus driver Fred Flange and also paid him £25 to sing on a Peter Sellers' album.

For the record the extraordinary assortment of artists who have covered 'Yesterday' – which Ringo rightly acknowledges as "the most recorded song in history" – includes Elvis (this time live in Vegas), Tammy Wynette, Placido Domingo, Tom Jones, The Seekers, Arthur Mullard, Acker Bilk, Sarah Vaughan, Marianne Faithfull, Dr John, Willie Nelson, the Supremes, Cilla Black, Perry Como, Boyz II Men, Nana Mouskouri, En Vogue, Otis Redding, Pat Boone … and Marvin Gaye, whose version is said to be among the composer's favourites.

Acknowledgements:

My thanks go to Mark Neeter, Red Planet and also to those people who gave their time and shared their thoughts with me. The music of The Beatles is something which almost all music lovers have an opinion about – thankfully.

Bibliography

All You Need Is Ears by George Martin (Macmillan 1979)
The Life & Times of Little Richard by Charles White (Omnibus 2003)
Chuck Berry (Faber & Faber 88)
The Beatles Anthology by The Beatles (Cassell & Co 2000)
Off The Record by Joe Smith (Pan 1988)
Many Years From Now by Miles (Secker & Warburg 1997)
Barefaced Lies & Boogie Woogie Boasts by Jools Holland (Penguin 2008)
John Paul George Ringo & Me by Tony Barrow (Andre Deutsch 2005)
Yesterday & Today by Ray Coleman (Boxtree 1995)
The Complete Guide To The Music Of The Beatles by John Robertson (Omnibus 1994)
The Beatles Album File & Complete Discography by Jeff Russell (Blandford Press 1982)
The Complete Beatles Recording Sessions by Mark Lewisohn (Hamlyn 1988)
The Beatles Encyclopedia by Bill Harry (Virgin 2000)
The Beatles Live by Mark Lewisohn (Pavilion 1986)
Cover Versions by Adam Sweeting (Pimlico 2004)
The Beatles Uncovered by Dave Henderson (Black Book Company 2000)
James Taylor: Long Ago And Far Away by Timothy White (Omnibus 2002)
Rolling Stone Interviews (Arthur Baker 1981)
Diamond Diva by Peter Hogan (Andre Deutsch 2008)

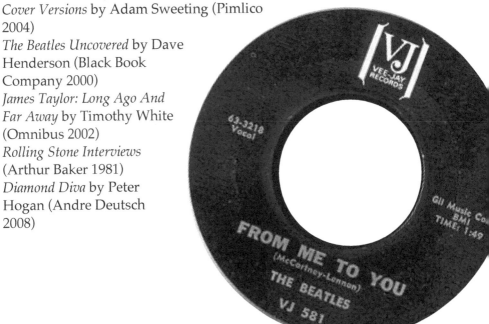

The musical landscape of America

650 GREAT MUSIC LOCATIONS

ROCK ATLAS USA

David Roberts

The musical landscape of America

Album cover & music video locations

Venues, festivals, studios, & homes

Statues, graves, museums, memorials, & plaques

Exclusive interviews and more than 500 fascinating photographs

Crosby, Stills & Nash Cover shoot by Henry Diltz, West Hollywood, 1969

PLUS! THE BRILL BUILDING • DEAD MAN'S CURVE • THE JOSHUA TREE • PAISLEY PARK • AND MORE

ROCK ATLAS is more than just a guide to 650 music locations across the USA. You can visit many of the places by following the book's detailed instructions or simply just enjoy reading the fascinating, fact-packed stories behind each entry.

Seek out the quirky record stores, find the iconic recording studios, make a pilgrimage to memorials and statues, check out the best festivals, and visit the exact spot where your favourite album cover was photographed. Rock Atlas USA will be your guide.

Providing a unique insight into musicians' lives and songs through the places linked to them, Rock Atlas USA includes stories featuring artists as diverse as The Beatles, Lady Gaga, Muddy Waters, Bruce Springsteen, Kings of Leon, and Otis Redding.

Illustrated with hundreds of rare, unseen, and iconic colour and black and white photographs, Rock Atlas USA is a must for anyone with an emotional tie to contemporary music and the important places associated with it.

On sale now in all good bookstores